Contents

CHAPTER 9

The Road to Healing 80

CHAPTER 10

Beyond Surviving 89

Your Child, Safe from Secrets

Second Edition — Revised & Updated

PUBLICATION HISTORY

First published: February 2019

Second edition, revised and updated: March 2026

DISCLAIMER

This book is intended for educational and informational purposes only. The content is not a substitute for professional medical, legal, or therapeutic advice. The author is a physician assistant and child safety advocate — not an attorney. Laws regarding child protection, mandatory reporting, and legal processes vary by state. For guidance specific to your situation, consult a qualified professional in your area.

RESOURCES & PROGRAMS

Crusader for Kids | www.tiffanysjohnson.com

Safe Talk Prevention Program | www.tiffanysjohnson.com

CONTACT

For speaking inquiries, organizational training, or bulk orders:

www.tiffanysjohnson.com

contact@crusaderforkids.com

A NOTE OF GRATITUDE

Acknowledgements

Writing a book has been one of the hardest and one of the most rewarding projects I have ever undertaken. If someone had told me that I would become an author, I would have looked at you like you were absolutely insane. I couldn't have completed this project without my circle of family, friends, and business associates.

First, I would like to thank my mom and dad, Patricia and James Shearn, for being my moral compass, prayer partners, advocates, and supporters. Mom, your daily encouragement means more than you will ever know and has gotten me through some rough times. You have stood by my side through everything in life, and I know you will continue to do so for all eternity. Daddy, you know you are my hero, and I thank you for encouraging me to be the best me that I can be. I love you both with all of my heart.

Next, I want to thank my sister and attorney, Beatrice Foster. I love you so much, and I have always admired the strong woman you are. Thank you for supporting me and helping me with all the business matters I knew nothing about. You are one bad mamma-jamma! I love you!

To my sweet, sassy, intelligent, beautiful babies, Kadence and Kyndall. Both of you are clear examples that God is in the miracle-working business. I thank God every day for trusting me to be your Mommy. I love you both with all of my being.

Lastly, I must say a huge thank you to my superman, my number one fan, my amazing husband, Ed. You are my greatest supporter and the steady hand behind everything I do. I'm so glad God answered my prayers when He made you just for me. When I told you I wanted to do something different, you didn't hesitate one bit and told me to "go for it, you will do well in whatever you choose to do." Thank you for having so much faith in me, for loving our family so fiercely, and for being the Yin to my Yang. You will forever be my King! I love you so much and appreciate all that you do for us!

— Tiffany Johnson, PA-C

Safe From Secrets

Tiffany Johnson, PA-C

2026 Second Edition — Revised & Updated

INTRODUCTION

A Personal Story

This is the fully revised and updated second edition of Your Child, Safe from Secrets, originally published in 2019.

Growing up in a huge family, I had lots of aunts, uncles, cousins, and an abundance of kids. We were a very close-knit family and would get together at my grandmother's house every Sunday evening after church for Sunday dinner. I grew up in the south, so this was a very common tradition.

My Grandmother, the matriarch of the family, taught us to love family and others wholeheartedly, especially those in need. Whenever we were together, I always felt as if nothing else mattered and everything in the world was right.

As we headed home after visiting family, it was our practice to hug all the adults prior to leaving. I never questioned this as a child because it was all I knew and it felt right. This was an act that expressed my love for my family and their love for me. My family were very loving and protective, and I never had to question the motives of the relatives in my grandmother's home or wonder whether that hug was out of place or inappropriate.

My mother was very vigilant in teaching my siblings and me about appropriate and inappropriate touching. She always made sure we knew it was okay for us to tell her or my dad if anyone crossed those boundaries.

From an early age, she taught us about our bodies using terms like private parts so we understood that no one was allowed to touch us there unless it was her or the doctor (and even then, only while she was present). When we were children I can remember Mom telling us to wear pants or shorts under our nightgowns when we were around my dad or brother.

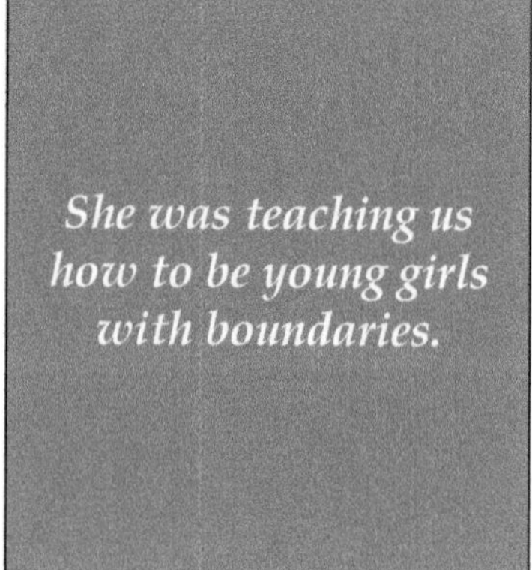

At the time I thought she was just being extra. She was being protective. There is a difference — and I did not fully appreciate it until I was grown.

I also recall that we were not allowed to sit on the laps of our uncles, male cousins, or family friends as it was seen as inappropriate. At the time I didn't understand the purpose of all of these rules, but as I write this book and see how many children are affected by sexual abuse, I totally get it.

I believe my mother's goal was to make sure there wasn't an opportunity created for something inappropriate to happen or for someone to try to take advantage of me. She was very protective of our innocence, and I am very grateful to her for that. Her actions may sound a bit overbearing to some, but as a kid I never really looked at it that way. I just thought she was teaching us how to be young girls with boundaries.

She always kept an eye on us and made sure we were never in harm's way. She knew that we wouldn't always be with her 24/7, so she taught us how to be cognizant of people around us and to listen to our intuition and tell someone if we were violated in any way. She made sure to do everything in her power to ensure there was little chance that we were molested or sexually abused.

Despite the protective measures my mother implemented, she couldn't completely shield us from men who had a propensity to prey on young girls. You know those men — the ones that immediately give off the creep factor as soon as you meet them. They seemed to always be around the spots where kids hang out, like the school (especially during sporting events), in the church, and even at family functions. They're the ones that hug for a little longer than what seemed appropriate or find a way to brush against you and then pretend it was a mistake.

One of my earliest experiences with a creepy guy was when I was 13 or 14 years old. It happened right in the middle of a church service. The pastor had just called for that familiar moment — "Turn and greet your neighbor, welcome them into the service"

— the kind of warm, communal moment that is supposed to feel safe. It is church, after all. This church member reached out to give me a hug, as church members sometimes do as a greeting. While he was hugging me, he proceeded to bend down and kiss me on the neck.

If it does not seem right, it probably isn't. Trust your instincts.

It happened so quickly, I was shocked and appalled that he would do something like that — and in the middle of the church. I was so embarrassed, and I immediately felt dirty and violated. Internally, I questioned, why did he do that? Did I do something to make him think it was ok to kiss me on my neck?

I looked at him with disbelief and pushed him away. I didn't tell my parents immediately because I figured I'd just stay away from him and make sure I didn't let him in my space again. I decided to try to forget about it. It was only after hearing my older sister say he did something similar to her that I decided to tell my parents what he did to me.

The only difference with my sister was that she immediately had the courage to tell him she was going to tell my dad about his behavior. I can't remember exactly what my Dad did at the time, but I knew he would handle the situation. From then on, we never had any issues with inappropriate behavior from that church member. Plus, I made sure to stay away from any physical contact outside of a handshake, and even that was rare.

Years later, as an adult, I found myself thinking back on that moment — and the more I sat with it, the more it disturbed me. Not just because of what happened, but because of where it happened. In church. In the middle of a service. In a room full of people. If someone felt emboldened enough to do that to me in plain sight — in a place that was supposed to be one of the safest in the world — I kept asking myself: what is happening to children behind closed doors? What is happening when there are no witnesses, no crowd, no one to push away from? How many children are enduring far worse right now, and never telling a single soul? That question would not leave me. And eventually, it became this book.

There are children in this world who endure much worse than what I experienced that day. Many of these kids are sexually abused daily, and many deal with it in silence and fear. These are the kids who need protecting the most.

How will these children receive the knowledge and help needed to protect them from being an easy target of sexual predators? Who will be there to protect the kids that have no family support, those who have no one willing to care for them? Who will take the time to teach them about their bodies and appropriate and inappropriate touching?

The safety of all children is important to me, and I have a responsibility as a medical provider to help educate parents, caregivers, and the organizations that serve children on how to keep them safe from the secrets of child sexual abuse. Children should experience unconditional love and be protected, empowered, and guided through childhood to become healthy adults.

Every child deserves to grow up in a world where the adults around them are prepared, informed, and committed to their protection.

Unfortunately, for many children this is not a reality, and I see evidence of that all too often in my job. For many children, their reality consists of living in fear, sometimes not knowing where they will find the next meal or who will care for them. They face a life of terror, distrust, unwantedness, loneliness, and worst of all — a life of abuse.

For these children, their world is hell on earth, and many suffer in silence. Child sexual abuse has reached epidemic proportions, and more needs to be done to bring awareness to the many kids that are affected. Understanding the prevalence, risk factors, and signs of child abuse will better prepare all of us to prevent more children from becoming victims and having to face the abuse on their own.

There's no shortage of cases in the headlines reporting children being sexually abused. Most times the abuser has some close relationship with the child, but other times it's an act committed by a stranger. My heart aches for any child who has experienced sexual abuse, but there is a unique pain when the perpetrator is a parent or guardian.

As parents, caregivers, community members, and leaders of the organizations that children trust — churches, schools, sports programs, youth camps — we have the responsibility to provide children with their basic needs. But more than that, we are responsible for giving them love, support, and protection so that they have the chance to grow into healthy adults. Even if you are not a parent, you can still play a major role in protecting the kids in your community.

This book is written for every adult who holds a child's world in their hands — parents, caregivers, and the organizational leaders those families trust. Whether you are raising children at home or leading the church, school, sports program, or youth organization where they spend their days, you have been given something extraordinary: the trust of a child. These pages will help you honor that trust with the knowledge, the conversations, and the culture to keep them safe. It will equip you to recognize the signs of abuse, understand how predators operate, and ensure that every child in your care knows what to do if something goes wrong.

My hope is that these pages empower rather than frighten — that after reading, you will feel equipped, not overwhelmed. Child sexual abuse is preventable when communities are educated, and it is survivable when survivors are believed and supported. Let's build that world together.

— Tiffany Johnson, PA-C

What Every Parent and Organization Needs to Know

Every twenty-three minutes, another child is sexually abused in the United States. That number is not a statistic pulled from a distant headline — it is happening in homes, schools, churches, sports programs, and youth organizations in every community in this country, including yours.

Fair warning: some of what you read in this chapter will be uncomfortable. That discomfort is intentional — and it is worth sitting with.

This chapter lays the groundwork. It gives you the honest picture of how widespread child sexual abuse really is, who is most often responsible, why children so rarely speak up, and what allows abuse to continue unchecked in communities and institutions that should know better. Some of what you read here will be uncomfortable. That discomfort is worth sitting with — because it is exactly the discomfort that most predators are counting on adults to avoid.

How Many Children Are Affected?

The scale of child sexual abuse in the United States is hard to fully absorb — and that is partly by design, because so much of it goes unreported. But the data we do have paints a sobering picture.

Think about the last group of children you were around. A classroom, a youth group, a sports team. According to the CDC, about one in four girls and one in thirteen boys will experience sexual abuse before their eighteenth birthday.[1] Sit with that for a moment. In a room of twenty girls, that is five children. On a boys' basketball team of thirteen players — that is one of them. These are not abstractions — they are the kids already in your life, some of whom may already be carrying something no child should carry alone.

> *Picture a classroom of 20 girls. Statistically, five of them will experience sexual abuse before they turn 18.*

And those numbers almost certainly undercount the truth. Because the majority of children who are sexually abused never tell anyone — not a parent, not a teacher, not a friend. The abuse lives inside them in silence, sometimes for decades. What we can measure is only what gets reported, and reporting is the exception, not the rule.

One more thing worth understanding: most of the sexual violence that occurs in this country happens to children, not adults. Nearly seven out of ten reported sexual assaults involve a victim who is seventeen or younger.[2] We often talk about sexual violence as an adult issue. The data says otherwise. This is, above all else, a children's crisis.

Who Is Actually Doing This?

Here is the thing that changes everything — and the thing most people do not want to believe.

It is not the stranger in the parking lot. It is not the creepy-looking man lurking near the playground. That number holds across virtually every study, every community, every demographic. It does not matter whether we are talking about affluent suburbs or rural towns — the pattern is the same. A family member, a family friend, a coach, a teacher, a youth pastor, a neighbor who has been welcomed into the home.[3] Someone who has earned trust. Someone who may have earned yours too.

> *Nine times out of ten, the person who abuses a child is someone that child already knows and trusts.*

This is why teaching children to "watch out for strangers" is not enough. Stranger danger is a real concept, but it addresses a small fraction of the actual threat. The more important conversations — the ones that actually protect children — are about body autonomy, about safe and unsafe touch, about the difference between a good secret and a bad secret, and about the fact that no adult should ever ask a child to keep a physical secret. We cover all of that in Chapter 6.

For you as a parent, caregiver, or organizational leader, this also means something harder: your circle is not automatically safe. Pay attention to the adult who always volunteers to be alone with a child. Notice the one who gives your child special gifts or attention without explanation. Watch how your child's body language changes around certain people. Your instincts matter. Use them.

How Caregivers Can Unknowingly Open the Door

This next part is not about blame. It is about information — because you cannot make protective decisions without it.

> *Convenience is not a safety plan. Knowing who has access to your child — and why — is.*

Federal research has found that children who live with a single parent and that parent's live-in partner face dramatically higher rates of abuse than children living with two biological parents.[4] This does not mean every blended family is unsafe, or that single parents are doing something wrong. What it means is that adults who are not biologically connected to a child warrant careful, intentional vetting before being given significant access to that child.

Predators who target children are often very deliberate about choosing homes where supervision may be reduced and a new adult's presence is normalized quickly. They look for opportunity. Removing or reducing that opportunity is one of the most practical things a parent can do. That means running background checks on babysitters, checking references, doing a second interview with your child present so you can watch how the two of them interact. It means trusting your gut when something feels off — even if you cannot name exactly why.

One of the most powerful protective tools you can give your child costs nothing: teach them from an early age that their body belongs to them. A child who has internalized that lesson — who knows they have the right to say no to any touch that makes them uncomfortable, even from family members, even from people they love — is a much harder target for a grooming predator. Chapter 6 walks you through exactly how to have these conversations at every age, from toddlerhood through the teenage years.

> *I want to be clear about something — I am not blaming single parents. I know exactly how hard that road is, and so do millions of families across this country. This section is about information, not indictment. Knowing the risk factors does not mean you caused them. It means you can do something about them.*

Boys Are Not Exempt — and They Need to Hear That

When we talk about child sexual abuse, the conversation tends to center on girls. That focus is understandable — girls are statistically abused at higher rates. But it leaves boys in a dangerous blind spot.

One in thirteen boys will be sexually abused before they turn eighteen.[1] And because boys face a particular layer of stigma — the expectation that they should be strong, that abuse is something that happens to girls, that a male victim of a male abuser must somehow be complicit — many will carry that experience without ever speaking a word about it. Some will not speak about it until they are middle-aged adults, if ever.

> *Boys need explicit permission to speak up — and they need to hear from the adults in their lives that abuse is not their fault, does not define them, and that real strength includes knowing when to ask for help.*

Boys who experience abuse may also be confused by their body's physical response to what happened. An involuntary physiological response does not mean they wanted the abuse or that they are in any way responsible for it. That confusion, if left unaddressed, becomes shame. And shame keeps children silent far longer than fear does.

The conversations we have with sons about body safety, consent, and appropriate touch are just as important as the ones we have with daughters. This book is written for both — and for the coaches, pastors, and teachers who often have more daily contact with boys than their parents do.

Why Children Do Not Tell

If your child was being abused, you would know. They would tell you. This is one of the most common assumptions parents make — and one of the most dangerous.

> *Most children who are sexually abused never tell a single person. Many carry it in silence for years. Some never speak about it at all.*

Research consistently shows that at least half of all child sexual abuse victims never disclose the abuse.[5] Of those who do eventually tell someone, many wait months or years, and they rarely tell the whole story at once. Disclosure happens gradually, in pieces, often only after testing whether an adult can be trusted with a smaller truth first. And if that test fails — if the adult reacts with panic, disbelief, or by minimizing what the child said — the child often goes back underground and does not try again.

The reasons children stay silent are real and deeply felt. They may have been threatened by the abuser. They may feel ashamed, or genuinely believe what happened was partly their fault — especially if the abuser groomed them carefully over time to feel that way. They may love the person who hurt them and not want to see them get in trouble. They may be terrified of breaking up their family. They may simply not have the words, particularly if they are very young.

What this means for you is straightforward: do not wait for your child to volunteer that something is wrong. Build the kind of relationship where they know — really know — that they can tell you anything without being punished, doubted, or causing you to fall apart. The chapters ahead will help you build exactly that foundation. Chapter 7 walks through what to do the moment a child does speak up, because your response in that moment can determine whether they keep talking or go silent again.

How Abuse Stays Hidden

Child sexual abuse survives because of silence — and that silence is not accidental. It is carefully maintained, both by the abuser and, often unknowingly, by the adults and institutions surrounding the child.

Let's start with a myth worth putting to rest: children almost never lie about being sexually abused. Research puts the rate of intentional false reports somewhere between two and eight

> *When a child tells you something happened, believe them first. The evidence says they are almost certainly telling the truth.*

percent — and most of those false reports are made by adults, not children, usually in the context of custody disputes.[6] When a child tells you something happened to them, every statistical indicator says they are telling the truth. Believing children is not naïve. It is accurate.

Yet families, faith communities, and institutions regularly respond to abuse disclosures in ways that protect the accused rather than the child. A mother stays with a partner because she cannot afford to leave, and the abuse continues. A youth pastor is quietly reassigned to another congregation because the church board does not want a scandal. A school district declines to report a teacher because it cannot afford the lawsuit. In each of these cases, the adult or institution made a choice — and a child paid the price for it.

The good news is that the opposite is equally true. When adults are educated, when institutions have real policies, when children are explicitly taught that their voice matters and will be heard — the opportunity for abuse shrinks dramatically. This book exists to help create exactly that kind of community.

A Direct Word to Organizations That Serve Children

If you are a pastor, school principal, youth sports director, camp administrator, or any kind of organizational leader — this is written for you specifically.

The children who walk through your doors every week are there because families trust you. That trust is not a formality — it is a genuine belief that your organization is a safe place. The question you need to be willing to ask yourself honestly is whether your policies actually back that up, or whether you are relying on good intentions and hoping for the best.

> *Good intentions are not a child protection policy. Written, enforced procedures are.*

Research shows that most child sexual abuse occurs in one-on-one settings — a single adult alone with a single child.[2] The simplest and most effective structural protection any organization can implement is to eliminate those situations. Two adults present whenever children are present. Open-door policies for any individual meeting between a child and an adult. Clear, immediate reporting protocols when something seems wrong. These are not burdensome — they are basic.

Chapter 11 of this book is dedicated entirely to helping your organization build a culture where children are genuinely safe. It covers background checks, staff training, reporting systems, and the kind of institutional transparency that actually deters predatory behavior. A predator who knows that your organization watches closely, reports consistently, and takes every concern seriously will look for a softer target. Make your organization the hard target.

The children in your care cannot protect themselves. They are counting on you to build something worthy of the trust their families placed in you.

R E F E R E N C E S

1. Centers for Disease Control and Prevention. (2024). Preventing Child Sexual Abuse. Retrieved from https://www.cdc.gov/violenceprevention/childsexualabuse

2. Darkness to Light. (2023). Child Sexual Abuse Statistics. Retrieved from https://www.d2l.org/the-issue/statistics/

3. RAINN. (2024). Children and Teens: Statistics. Retrieved from https://www.rainn.org/statistics/children-and-teens

4. U.S. Department of Health and Human Services. (2010). Fourth National Incidence Study of Child Abuse and Neglect (NIS–4). Retrieved from https://www.acf.hhs.gov

5. Darkness to Light. (2023). Child Sexual Abuse Disclosure Research. Retrieved from https://www.d2l.org

6. London, K., Bruck, M., Ceci, S., & Shuman, D. (2005). Disclosure of child sexual abuse. Psychology, Public Policy, and Law, 11(1), 194–226.

More Than a Touch — Understanding What Child Sexual Abuse Really Is

When most people hear the words "child sexual abuse," their mind goes to one thing. Physical contact. Rape. Penetration. Something violent and unmistakable. And while those things are absolutely part of this conversation, defining abuse that narrowly is one of the reasons so much of it goes unrecognized — and unreported.

This chapter breaks it down clearly — what the law and research define as child sexual abuse, the different forms it takes, how it typically unfolds over time, and why some of the most harmful forms of exploitation are the ones we talk about least. Knowledge is not just power here. It is protection.

What Child Sexual Abuse Actually Is

Child sexual abuse (CSA) is any sexual activity involving a child who is unable to fully understand what is happening, unable to give informed consent, or who is being manipulated or coerced by someone older or in a position of power. It is

> *Abuse does not have to involve physical touch to cause deep, lasting harm to a child.*

not defined by the child's reaction. It is not defined by whether the child said no. It is not defined by whether the child seemed distressed. A child cannot consent to sexual activity with an adult — full stop. That is true regardless of how the child responded, regardless of how the abuser framed it, and regardless of whether physical force was used.

The World Health Organization defines it this way: the involvement of a child in sexual activity that they do not fully comprehend, are unable to give informed consent to, or for which they are not developmentally prepared — including any activity that violates the laws or social norms of their society.[1] What matters in that definition is not what happened to the child's body. What matters is whether the child had the capacity to genuinely understand and agree. They do not. They cannot. And any adult who proceeds anyway is committing abuse.

Contact Abuse: When There Is Physical Touch

Contact abuse is what most people picture — and it is exactly what it sounds like. It involves any sexual activity where there is physical contact between the abuser and the child. This includes:

- Fondling or touching a child's genitals, breasts, or buttocks — over or under clothing — for the purpose of sexual gratification
- Oral-to-genital contact in either direction
- Vaginal or anal penetration with any body part or object
- Forcing or encouraging a child to touch the abuser's body sexually
- Kissing of a sexual nature
- Any physical sexual act performed on a child, or that a child is directed to perform

Forcible fondling is actually the most commonly reported form of contact abuse — more common than penetration. That matters because it is also the form most likely to be minimized or dismissed. "He just touched her" is a phrase that has allowed abusers to escape accountability, and it reflects a fundamental misunderstanding of what abuse does to a child. Any unwanted sexual contact leaves a mark — not necessarily on the body, but always on the child.

Non-Contact Abuse: No Touch Required

This is the category that surprises people most — and the one that most often goes unrecognized. Non-contact sexual abuse involves no physical touch between the abuser and the child, but it is still abuse, it is still a crime, and it causes real psychological harm.

> **Exhibitionism**
>
> An adult exposing their genitals to a child for sexual gratification. This is a crime regardless of whether the child appeared frightened or indifferent.

> **Voyeurism**
>
> An adult watching a child undress, bathe, or engage in any private activity for sexual gratification — including hidden cameras in bedrooms or bathrooms.

> **Exposure to pornography**
>
> Showing a child sexually explicit material — whether to desensitize them, to demonstrate what the abuser wants the child to do, or for the abuser's own gratification. This is often a step in the grooming process.

> **Sexual communication**
>
> Sending or receiving sexually explicit messages, images, or videos involving a child — via text, apps, social media, or any online platform. This includes sexting between an adult and a minor, even if the child initiated it.

> **Sexual harassment**
>
> Repeated, unwanted sexual comments, gestures, or behavior directed at a child, including from peers. This is often dismissed as "kids being kids" — it is not.

> **Taking sexualized images**
>
> Photographing or filming a child in a sexual way — even if the child is clothed. This includes any image intended to be used for sexual purposes.

Non-contact abuse is not a lesser category. Abusers often use it as a deliberate first step — gauging the child's reaction, testing boundaries, desensitizing the child to sexual content before escalating to physical contact. Recognizing it for what it is, and taking it seriously when a child discloses it, can interrupt an abuser's path before physical harm occurs. Showing a child pornography, exposing yourself to them, or watching them undress — these are all forms of sexual abuse, even without a single touch.

> *I want to pause here because this is where a lot of people get it wrong. Non-contact abuse gets minimized. 'He didn't actually touch her.' 'Nothing really happened.' But I have sat with families dealing with the aftermath of non-contact abuse and I can tell you — something happened. The damage is real. The shame is real. Do not let anyone — including yourself — talk you out of taking it seriously.*

How Abuse Typically Unfolds: The Grooming Process

Child sexual abuse rarely begins with a sudden assault. In the overwhelming majority of cases — particularly those involving someone the child knows — it builds gradually through a process called grooming. Understanding grooming is one of the most important things a parent, caregiver, or organizational leader can do, because it is what makes abuse possible, and it is what makes it so hard for children to name what is happening to them.

> *Grooming is a deliberate, calculated process. By the time abuse begins, the child often does not recognize it as abuse at all.*

Grooming begins with target selection. Predators are not random. They look for children who appear vulnerable — kids who are isolated, who seem to be starved for attention and affirmation, who come from chaotic home environments, or who are simply easier to access and control. A child whose parent is frequently absent is a more accessible target. A child who lights up when given special attention is easier to manipulate. This is not the child's fault — or the parent's fault in most cases. It is the abuser making a calculated choice.

Once a target is identified, the abuser works to insert themselves into the child's life and gain the trust of the adults around them. They volunteer to help. They are generous. They are reliable. They build a reputation as someone who is good with kids. Parents relax around them — sometimes even nudge their child to spend more time with this wonderful adult who takes such an interest. This is by design.

Next comes the isolation phase. The abuser looks for opportunities to spend one-on-one time with the child, away from other adults. A car ride. A tutoring session with the door closed. A camping trip. A sleepover. Offering to babysit when the parent is in a bind. The goal is to remove the protective buffer of other adults so the abuser has full control of the interaction.

Once alone access is established, the abuser begins sexualizing the relationship — slowly, carefully, in ways that can be plausibly explained away. An accidental brush. A joke that crosses a line. Showing the child something online. Introducing physical contact gradually, always watching for the child's reaction, always ready to frame it as playful or affectionate if needed.

By the time overt abuse begins, the child is often confused. They may care about this person. They may have accepted gifts, special treatment, and affection from them. The abuser has worked hard to make the child feel that they are participants in a special relationship — not victims of a crime. When the abuse is eventually named for what it is, children frequently feel shame, complicity, and loyalty to the abuser all at once. That is not an accident. That is the grooming process working exactly as designed.

> *When I learned how deliberate and patient the grooming process actually is, it made me furious. Not at the children who were manipulated — at the adults who should have been paying closer attention. Grooming works because we want to believe the best about the people around us. That is a human instinct and there is nothing wrong with it. But protecting children requires us to stay curious even when everything looks fine. The question is never 'do I trust this person?' The question is 'does my child have the tools and the permission to tell me if something goes wrong?'*

For organizations that serve children: grooming does not only target children. It targets adults too. An abuser who is working their way into a youth program will also invest heavily in charming leadership, building goodwill with staff, and making themselves indispensable to the organization. The two-adult rule and open-door policies discussed in Chapter 11 are specifically designed to interrupt the isolation phase that grooming requires.

Child Exploitation: When Abuse Becomes Commerce

Child sexual exploitation refers to situations in which a child is manipulated or coerced into sexual activity in exchange for something — money, food, shelter, drugs, affection, or perceived love and safety. It is abuse that has been monetized, and it is far more common and far closer to home than most people want to believe.

> *Sex trafficking does not happen somewhere else. It happens in our cities, our suburbs, and sometimes in homes that look completely ordinary.*

Sex trafficking is the most visible form of child exploitation in the news, and many people picture it as foreign girls being kidnapped and shipped overseas. The reality is far less dramatic in appearance and far more devastating in prevalence. Children are commercially sexually exploited in every major American city, in mid-sized towns, in suburbs. They are sold by people they know —

sometimes by family members, sometimes by boyfriends or older friends who presented themselves as protectors. The average age of entry into commercial sexual exploitation is between twelve and fourteen years old. Some victims are younger.[2]

These children are not there by choice, even when it looks that way. A fourteen-year-old who has run away from an abusive home, who hasn't eaten in two days, who has an older man offering her food and a place to sleep and someone who says he loves her — that child is not making a free choice. She is surviving. Understanding that distinction is the difference between treating a victim like a criminal and getting her the help she actually needs.

Online exploitation has grown dramatically alongside the rise of smartphones and social media. A child does not have to leave their bedroom to be exploited. They can be manipulated into producing sexual images from their own device, threatened with exposure if they do not continue, and that content can circulate online indefinitely. Images shared once are essentially permanent. That child may be living with the consequences of a single exploitative interaction for the rest of their life.

Child Sexual Abuse Material: Abuse That Lives Forever

The term "child pornography" is technically accurate but dangerously misleading — it sounds like a content category rather than what it actually is: documented evidence of a child being sexually abused. Many advocates and researchers now prefer the term child sexual abuse material (CSAM) because it more accurately reflects what these images represent. There is nothing pornographic about them in the consensual-adult sense.

> *Every image of child sexual abuse material is a crime scene. A real child was harmed to produce it.*

They are records of crimes committed against children.

Every image or video in circulation represents a real child who was abused. Every view, download, or share of that material is a continuation of that child's victimization. Children depicted in these images are re-harmed every time someone accesses them — a fact that many victims carry with them into adulthood, knowing their abuse is still being watched somewhere, by someone, at any given moment.

The production, distribution, possession, and viewing of child sexual abuse material is a federal crime in the United States, prosecuted aggressively by the FBI, the National Center for Missing and Exploited Children, and the Internet Crimes Against Children Task Force. If you encounter this material online, report it immediately to the NCMEC CyberTipline at 1-800-843-5678 or cybertipline.org. Do not share it. Do not save it. Report it.

For parents: the most important thing to understand about CSAM is that it does not stay in a separate, sealed corner of the internet. Children who use smartphones and social media can encounter it. Abusers use it deliberately — showing it to children as part of the grooming process, to normalize sexual activity and lower the child's resistance. If your child mentions seeing something disturbing online involving other children, take it seriously, stay calm, and ask open questions. Chapter 6 covers how to have these conversations in age-appropriate ways.

Everything in this chapter may feel heavy. It is heavy. I do not present it to frighten you — I present it because you cannot protect children from things you cannot name. Every family that finishes this chapter and truly understands the full spectrum of abuse is a harder target for every predator counting on adults to look the other way. You just got more equipped. That matters more than you know.

R E F E R E N C E S

1. World Health Organization. (2023). Child Maltreatment Fact Sheet. Retrieved from https://www.who.int/news-room/fact-sheets/detail/child-maltreatment

2. National Center for Missing and Exploited Children. (2024). Child Sex Trafficking. Retrieved from https://www.missingkids.org/theissues/trafficking

3. RAINN. (2024). Child Sexual Abuse. Retrieved from https://www.rainn.org/articles/child-sexual-abuse

4. Internet Watch Foundation / NCMEC. (2023). CyberTipline Annual Report. Retrieved from https://www.missingkids.org/cybertipline

C H A P T E R

3

Who's Most at Risk

This chapter walks through the factors that research has consistently linked to elevated risk. Some will be familiar. Others may surprise you. All of them are worth understanding — because the child in your life who carries the most risk factors is also the one most likely to be carrying this alone.

Age: When Children Are Most Vulnerable

Child sexual abuse can happen at any age. Infants have been victimized. Adults have been victimized in ways that began in childhood. But the data shows a consistent pattern: children between the ages of seven and thirteen are at the highest statistical risk.[1] This is the window when children are old enough to be left in the care of others but not yet old enough to fully understand what is appropriate and inappropriate, or to feel confident enough to report it.

Children between the ages of 7 and 13 face the highest statistical risk — but abuse can begin in infancy and continue through adolescence.

For younger children — those under six — abuse tends to occur inside the home and during daytime hours, often by a caregiver. As children grow older and spend more time outside the home at school, in sports, at church, and in after-school programs, the location of abuse shifts accordingly. School-aged children and adolescents are more likely to be abused outside the home, during after-school hours, by someone connected to those activities.

The practical takeaway is not to panic at every age and stage — it is to make sure the protective conversations you are having are consistent, ongoing, and age-appropriate. A single talk about body safety when your child is five does not carry them through adolescence. These conversations need to happen again and again, evolving as your child grows. Chapter 6 gives you a roadmap for exactly that.

Gender: Understanding the Differences

Girls are sexually abused at higher rates than boys across virtually every study and data set. The highest risk period for girls is between twelve and fourteen, and the crimes committed against them tend to be more severe — forcible rape and assault occur at higher rates among female victims. Girls are also more likely to be abused over a longer duration.

Both girls and boys are at risk. The critical difference is how willing the world is to believe them when they speak up.

Boys face a different but equally serious set of risks. They are less likely to disclose — and when they do, they are statistically less likely to be believed, less likely to receive services, and more likely to encounter skepticism from the adults around them. The stigma around male victimization runs deep, and it runs in both directions: boys may feel that being abused makes them weak, and adults may unconsciously resist believing that a boy could be victimized. Neither is true. Neither is acceptable.

Transgender and gender-nonconforming youth face elevated risk on multiple fronts — they experience higher rates of abuse overall, they face greater barriers to disclosure, and they are less likely to receive affirming, appropriate support when they do come forward. Any organization that serves children needs to be prepared to respond with sensitivity and competence to a child of any gender identity.

Family Structure and Home Environment

Federal research has consistently found that a child's family structure and home environment are among the most significant predictors of sexual abuse risk. Children who live with both biological parents face the lowest rates of abuse. As the family structure changes — a parent leaves, a new partner enters, oversight becomes inconsistent — that risk rises, sometimes dramatically.[2]

> *A child's home environment is one of the strongest predictors of abuse risk — not because of what families look like from the outside, but because of what happens inside.*

Children who live with a single parent and that parent's live-in partner face more than ten times the rate of sexual abuse compared to children in two-biological-parent homes. This is not a condemnation of single parents — many single parents are doing extraordinary work under difficult circumstances, and the overwhelming majority of their partners are not abusers. What this data tells us is that any adult who enters a child's home and is given significant, unsupervised access — without the biological protective instinct and without adequate vetting — represents a risk that deserves deliberate, honest attention. If you are a single parent reading this, the question to ask is not whether to trust your partner. It is whether your child has been taught what appropriate and inappropriate adult behavior looks like, whether your child knows they can tell you anything without fear, and whether you have ever had that conversation with them directly.

Children in foster care carry one of the highest risk profiles of any population. Removed from their original families, often having already experienced trauma, and cycling through placements that may not be adequately screened or supervised, these children are extraordinarily vulnerable. Organizations that work with foster youth need specialized training in trauma-informed care and heightened awareness of the signs of ongoing abuse.

Parental mental illness, substance abuse, and domestic violence in the home all increase a child's risk — not because parents in those circumstances are abusers, but because those circumstances reduce supervision, increase chaos, and create the kind of vulnerability that predators look for. Supporting struggling families is not separate from child protection work. It is child protection work.

Children with Disabilities

Children with physical, cognitive, developmental, or communication-related disabilities face dramatically elevated rates of sexual abuse. Research estimates that these children are approximately three to four times more likely to be sexually abused than children without disabilities — and that number climbs even higher for children with mental health diagnoses and multiple disabilities.[3]

Children with disabilities are three to four times more likely to be sexually abused — and far less likely to receive appropriate support afterward.

Several factors drive this disparity. Children with disabilities often require intimate physical care from caregivers, creating both access and power dynamics that can be exploited. They may be less able to recognize inappropriate behavior, less able to articulate what has happened to them, and less likely to be believed when they do disclose. Their social isolation — which is already more common among disabled youth — reduces the number of protective adults in their lives.

The response system frequently fails these children as well. Law enforcement and medical providers may not be trained to interview a child with autism or a child who uses alternative communication. The result is that disabled children are abused more often, disclose less, and receive less support when they do — a compounding injustice that demands a direct response from every organization that serves this population.

Organizations that work with children with disabilities need to invest in specialized training for staff on appropriate boundaries, how to recognize signs of abuse in children who may not verbalize it, and creating reporting systems that are accessible regardless of a child's communication method.

Neglect, Isolation, and the Children No One Is Watching

Parental neglect and social isolation are among the most significant and least discussed risk factors for child sexual abuse. A child who is not being adequately supervised, who does not have consistent, caring adults watching out for them, is a child who is accessible. And accessibility is what predators look for above almost everything else.

Neglect takes many forms. Sometimes it looks like a child left alone for extended periods because a parent is working multiple jobs and there is no other option. Sometimes it looks like emotional neglect — a child who is physically present in the home but starved for attention and affirmation, and therefore far more susceptible to an adult who offers it. Sometimes it looks like a child whose parents are so consumed by their own struggles that the child has effectively been left to parent themselves.

> *I want to stay here for a moment because families skip over this section thinking it does not apply to them. Neglect does not always look like what we see on the news. Sometimes it looks like a high-functioning household where everyone is stretched thin and nobody is really paying attention. That child is still at risk. Accessibility is what predators prioritize above almost everything else — and busyness creates it.*

Children who are socially isolated — who have few friends, who are excluded by peers, who spend most of their time alone — are also at elevated risk. They have fewer protective relationships and fewer people who might notice if something has changed. The child who withdraws from activities they used to enjoy, who stops talking about school or friends, who seems to be carrying something heavy — that child needs an adult to ask a gentle question and mean it.

Runaway and Homeless Youth

Runaway and homeless youth represent one of the most acutely at-risk populations for sexual abuse and exploitation. Many of these young people left home because of abuse that was already happening — and found themselves in environments where it continued in different forms. Research suggests that nearly half of runaway youth have experienced sexual abuse prior to leaving home.[4]

A child living on the streets is not free. They are surviving — and survival often comes at a devastating cost.

On the streets, survival sex becomes a grim reality for many unaccompanied youth. Exchanging sexual contact for food, shelter, money, or protection is not a choice made freely — it is a choice made under conditions of desperation, and it is legally recognized as exploitation regardless of whether the young person agreed. The adults who facilitate or participate in that exchange are committing crimes, even when they frame it as an arrangement.

Organizations that work with homeless and runaway youth — shelters, drop-in centers, outreach programs — are on the front lines of this issue. Staff in these settings need clear, trauma-informed protocols for identifying signs of ongoing exploitation, for building trust with young people who have every reason not to trust adults, and for connecting them with services without further traumatizing them.

Internet Use and Digital Vulnerability

Online access has transformed the landscape of child sexual abuse in ways that are still being fully understood. The fundamental dynamic — an adult seeking access to a child, building trust over time, exploiting vulnerability — is not new. What is new is the reach, the speed, and the anonymity that digital platforms provide to people who want to harm children.

> *A predator with a smartphone can reach your child in their own bedroom. The internet removes the geographic barriers from dangers that have always existed.*

Adolescents between twelve and seventeen are the most common targets of online predators, and girls in that age range face the highest risk.[5] But younger children are increasingly targeted as well, as smartphones and tablets become part of daily life at earlier ages. Teaching children what to do when something uncomfortable happens online — stop, do not respond, and come tell me immediately — is one of the most important digital safety lessons you will ever give them. Make sure they have heard it more than once.

Geotagging is a specific and underappreciated risk. When a child posts a photo taken at their school, their home, or a regular hangout, that photo may be broadcasting their precise location to anyone who views it. Teaching children to turn off location services for apps and photos is a small, practical step with significant protective value. Chapter 6 covers the full range of digital safety conversations and exactly how to have them at every age.

R E F E R E N C E S

1. Finkelhor, D. (2012). Characteristics of Crimes Against Juveniles. Durham, NH: Crimes Against Children Research Center.

2. U.S. Department of Health and Human Services. (2010). Fourth National Incidence Study of Child Abuse and Neglect (NIS–4). Retrieved from https://www.acf.hhs.gov

3. Vera Institute of Justice. (2012). Sexual Abuse of People with Disabilities. Retrieved from https://www.vera.org

4. National Runaway Safeline. (2023). Runaway Youth Statistics. Retrieved from https://www.1800runaway.org

5. Crimes Against Children Research Center. (2023). Online Victimization of Youth. Retrieved from https://www.unh.edu/ccrc

C H A P T E R

4

Recognizing the Behavior

If this chapter makes you want to reevaluate a few people in your child's circle — good. That is exactly the right response to what you are about to read.

This chapter covers how predators gain access to children, what the grooming process looks like step by step, and the warning signs — in both adults and children — that every parent, caregiver, and organizational leader needs to know. The goal is not to make you suspicious of every kind adult in your child's life. It is to give you the knowledge to tell the difference between genuine care and calculated access.

Who Offenders Are — and What Actually Matters

Researchers who study child sexual offenders have identified patterns in how they think and operate. Some offenders do not have a primary attraction to children at all — they abuse because of circumstance, opportunity, or a moment of weakness, often combined with substance abuse or a chaotic personal life. Others deliberately seek children out as their primary preference, investing significant time and effort

> *Predators do not have a look. But they do have patterns — and learning those patterns is one of the most protective things you can do.*

into gaining access through trusted roles — coaching, teaching, youth ministry, childcare. What matters for your purposes is not which category an offender falls into. What matters is that both types look ordinary, both use the same grooming tactics, and both rely on the adults around them failing to recognize the warning signs. The detailed profiles of offender types are included in the appendix at the back of this book for readers who want to go deeper.

> *For a detailed breakdown of offender behavioral profiles — including situational, preferential, opportunistic, and coercive types — see Appendix B: Understanding Offender Profiles.*

Grooming: How Predators Build Access Over Time

Grooming is the deliberate process by which an offender gains the trust of a child — and the adults around that child — in order to create the conditions for abuse. It is not impulsive. It is calculated. And it is one of the primary reasons that most child sexual abuse goes undetected for so long.

> *Grooming is not a single act. It is a long, careful process — and by the time it is complete, the child often does not know abuse has begun.*

Understanding grooming is critical for every adult who works with or cares for children — not just parents. Coaches, teachers, youth pastors, and organizational leaders are often on the receiving end of grooming behavior directed at them, not just at the child. Predators invest in adult relationships precisely because a trusted adult is a much more effective cover than a suspicious one.

Step One: Identifying the Target

Predators are rarely random. They look for children who appear available, vulnerable, and unlikely to tell. A child who is hungry for adult attention. A child whose parents are absent, distracted, or struggling. A child who is socially isolated and would value a special friendship. Online, they look for children posting late at night, responding to strangers, or sharing personal details publicly. The selection process can be quick or it can be a slow, patient scan across an entire school, church, or sports program.

Step Two: Gaining Trust

Once a target is identified, the offender works to insert themselves into the child's world and build trust with the adults around them. They offer to help. They show up consistently. They are generous with time, attention, and sometimes money or gifts. They make themselves useful — babysitting when a single parent is in a bind, staying after practice to help a struggling athlete, volunteering for the roles no one else wants. To the adults around them, they look like a gift. That reputation is intentional.

Step Three: Filling a Need

The most effective grooming happens when the offender identifies what the child is lacking and becomes the person who provides it. For a child who craves attention, they offer praise and special notice. For a child who feels like an outsider, they offer belonging. For a child whose home is chaotic, they offer calm and predictability. For a teenager who feels unseen, they offer the feeling of being truly understood. This is not accidental — it is the core mechanism of grooming, and it is why the child often develops genuine affection for the person who is systematically manipulating them.

> *The most effective predators do not force their way into a child's life. They fill a vacancy that was already there.*

Step Four: Creating Isolation

Once trust is established with both the child and the surrounding adults, the offender moves to create one-on-one time with the child. A car ride home from practice. A special outing as a reward. Tutoring sessions with a closed door. Overnight trips. Babysitting. The goal is to remove the child from the protective buffer of other adults so the offender has full control. This is the stage where two-adult policies and open-door rules are most powerful — they make this step significantly harder to execute. An organization that eliminates one-on-one access eliminates the predator's single most essential tool.

Step Five: Desensitization

With private access established, the offender begins normalizing physical contact and sexual content gradually. Wrestling or tickling that goes slightly too far. A hug that lingers a moment too long. A joke with a sexual undercurrent. Showing the child content online and watching their reaction. Each small boundary crossing is a test — of the child's response, and of the adult world's awareness. If no one says anything, the next step becomes possible. The progression is slow and deliberate, and by the time overt sexual contact begins, the child has often been so carefully prepared that they do not immediately recognize it as abuse.

Step Six: Maintaining Silence

Once abuse begins, the offender shifts to keeping the child silent. The child may be told that what is happening is their fault, that they wanted it, that no one will believe them if they tell. They may be threatened with harm to themselves or their family. They may be told that disclosure will destroy the family or send the person they care about to prison. Because the child has been carefully groomed to feel loyalty and affection toward the offender, many of these tactics land with devastating effectiveness. The child stays silent not because they are weak — but because they have been systematically manipulated into doing so.

Warning Signs in Adults: What to Watch For

Grooming behavior has observable signs — but only if adults know what to look for. The following patterns, especially in combination, should prompt closer attention and direct action when warranted:

- Consistently seeks one-on-one time with a child, especially without clear reason or parental knowledge
- Gives a child special gifts, money, or privileges without the parents' awareness or consent
- Shows an unusual level of physical affection — excessive hugging, kissing, tickling, or touching
- Insists on physical affection from a child even when the child resists or seems uncomfortable
- Frequently communicates with a child privately via text, social media, or gaming platforms
- Takes photographs or videos of children without clear, legitimate reason
- Makes sexual jokes, comments, or innuendos around children
- Walks in on children while they are dressing or bathing without treating it as a serious boundary violation
- Expresses excessive interest in a child's physical development or sexuality
- Seems more comfortable and engaged with children than with adults in social settings
- Works to undermine a child's relationship with their parents or other trusted adults
- Creates situations where they are reliably alone with a child — volunteering for every car ride, every overnight, every solo supervision opportunity

No single item on this list is proof of abuse. But a pattern of these behaviors — particularly when combined with secretiveness, boundary violations, and the special treatment of one particular child — is a serious warning sign that warrants attention and action. Chapter 7 covers exactly what to do when you notice these signs, including how to talk to a child and when to involve authorities.

Warning Signs in Children: When Behavior Changes

Children who are being groomed or abused often cannot or will not say so directly. What they can do — and frequently do — is show it. Behavioral changes are often the first and only signal that something is wrong. They may be subtle, easy to dismiss as ordinary childhood difficulty. But when multiple changes appear together, or when they are sudden and unexplained, they deserve serious attention.

When a child's behavior shifts without a clear reason, that shift is a message. The question is whether there is an adult paying close enough attention to receive it.

Watch for a child who has become withdrawn from activities they previously loved. A child who suddenly avoids a particular person or place without being willing to say why. A child who is having nightmares, wetting the bed after having been dry for years, or showing other signs of regression. A child whose mood has shifted dramatically — who has become angry, clingy, flat, or fearful in ways that feel new and unexplained.

Older children and adolescents may show different signals — a sudden drop in school performance, new and unexplained gifts or money, withdrawal from friends and family, or the emergence of an intense, secretive relationship with an older person. They may begin using sexual language or exhibiting sexual behaviors that are beyond what is developmentally expected for their age. They may seem to be carrying something — a heaviness, a guardedness, a distance — that was not there before.

None of these signs, taken alone, means a child is being abused. Children go through difficult periods for all kinds of reasons. But they are worth noticing, worth asking about gently, and worth taking seriously when they persist. Chapter 5 covers the full range of behavioral and physical signs of abuse in detail, and Chapter 7 tells you exactly how to respond when you see them.

R E F E R E N C E S

1. Ramsland, K. & McGrain, P. (2010). Inside the Minds of Sexual Predators. Praeger.

2. Darkness to Light. (2023). Recognizing Grooming Behavior. Retrieved from https://www.d2l.org

3. Stop It Now. (2024). Warning Signs in Adults. Retrieved from https://www.stopitnow.org

4. Child Welfare Information Gateway. (2023). Parenting a Child Who Has Been Sexually Abused. Retrieved from https://www.childwelfare.gov

Reading the Signs

This chapter covers the full range of signs that may indicate a child is being sexually abused: emotional and behavioral changes, physical indicators, and the developmental context that helps distinguish normal childhood behavior from something that warrants closer attention. The goal is not to turn you into someone who sees abuse everywhere. It is to make sure you never miss it when it is right in front of you.

Why Physical Signs Are the Exception, Not the Rule

One of the most common misconceptions about child sexual abuse is that it always leaves physical evidence. In the majority of cases it does not — and this is not because the abuse was minor. It is because the body heals quickly, and because many forms of abuse leave no physical mark at all. The tissues of the anogenital region (the genital and anal area) have a rich blood supply and recover from trauma rapidly, often within days. By the time a medical examination takes place — which is frequently weeks or months after abuse began — there may be nothing physically visible to document.

> *A normal physical exam does not mean abuse did not happen. The absence of injury is not the absence of harm.*

Medical providers who specialize in child sexual abuse evaluations are trained to understand this. A normal exam is not a clean bill of health. It does not mean the child is lying, and it does not mean abuse did not occur. What it means is that physical evidence is time-sensitive and often absent even in confirmed cases of abuse. This is why behavioral signs — the things a child shows rather than says — are so critical for parents, caregivers, and organizational staff to understand.

> *If you suspect recent abuse — within the last 72 hours — take the child to a medical provider or emergency department immediately. Evidence collection is time-sensitive. Do not bathe the child or wash their clothing before the exam.*

Healthy Sexual Development: Knowing What's Normal

Before identifying signs of abuse, it helps to understand what normal sexual development looks like in children. Children are naturally curious about their bodies and the bodies of others. That curiosity is healthy and expected — and it does not, by itself, indicate anything concerning. The question is always whether a child's behavior is consistent with what is developmentally typical for their age, or whether it has crossed into territory that warrants attention.

AGES 2–5	AGES 6–12	AGES 13–17
TYPICAL	TYPICAL	TYPICAL
→ Curiosity about body parts	→ Questions about pregnancy and sex	→ Romantic and sexual interest in peers
→ Correct names for genitals	→ Experimenting with same-age peers	→ Masturbation in private
→ Touching own genitals at home	→ Masturbation in private	→ Experimenting with age-appropriate partners
→ Showing private parts with peers	→ Interest in romantic relationships	→ Questions about contraception
→ Interest in where babies come from	→ Awareness of sexual media content	→ Voyeuristic interest in others

CONCERNING	CONCERNING	CONCERNING
→ Sexual knowledge beyond experience → Sexual contact with other children → Inserting objects into genitals → Compulsive masturbation → Adult-like sexual role play	→ Explicit sexual knowledge beyond age → Asking adults to join sexual acts → Public or compulsive masturbation → Sexual drawings with graphic content	→ Sexual interest in younger children → Using force or substances for compliance → Asking adults for sexual contact → Compulsive sexual behavior

The items in the "concerning" columns do not automatically mean a child has been abused — but they do mean something is worth exploring. A child who is showing sexual knowledge or behavior far beyond their developmental stage has encountered that content somewhere. The conversation that follows that observation matters enormously.

Emotional and Behavioral Signs of Abuse

Emotional and behavioral changes are typically the earliest and most consistent indicators that something is wrong in a child's life. They may appear gradually, building over weeks or months as abuse continues. They may appear suddenly following a specific incident. And they may look, on the surface, like ordinary childhood struggles — which is exactly why they so often go unaddressed for so long.

The following changes, particularly when they appear in combination or persist over time without a clear explanation, are worth taking seriously:

EMOTIONAL CHANGES	BEHAVIORAL CHANGES
→ Sudden withdrawal from people or activities they previously enjoyed	→ Regression to earlier behaviors — bedwetting, thumb-sucking, baby talk
→ Unexplained anger, irritability, or rage	→ Clinging to a parent or refusing to separate
→ Persistent sadness, flatness, or loss of interest	→ Avoiding a specific person or place without being able to explain why
→ New or intensifying fears — of the dark, of being alone, of specific people	→ Decline in school performance or sudden disengagement
→ Low self-esteem, self-hatred, or expressions of feeling worthless	→ Self-harm — cutting, burning, scratching
→ Anxiety, hypervigilance, or being easily startled	→ Running away or not wanting to go home
→ Expressions of hopelessness or thoughts of suicide	→ Increased risky behavior — substance use, sexual risk-taking
→ Guilt or shame without a clear reason	→ Giving away possessions or saying goodbye

A single item from this list, in isolation, is not cause for alarm. What matters is pattern and persistence — multiple signs appearing together, changes that do not have another clear explanation, or behaviors that are worsening rather than resolving over time.

Physical Signs: What to Know

As noted earlier, most children who have been sexually abused will not show physical signs. But in cases where physical contact was recent, forceful, or repeated over a long period, certain findings may be present. No parent or caregiver should attempt to examine a child themselves or draw conclusions from what they observe. If you see any of the following, contact a medical provider or take the child to an emergency department:

> *Physical findings are rare — but when they are present, they must be evaluated by a trained medical provider immediately.*

- Unexplained bleeding, bruising, or injury in the genital, anal, or inner thigh area
- Vaginal discharge, redness, or irritation not explained by hygiene or a known medical condition
- Difficulty walking or sitting without a clear physical explanation
- Complaints of pain, itching, or burning in the genital or anal area
- Urinary tract infections in young children, particularly if recurrent
- Sexually transmitted infections in a child or adolescent
- Pregnancy in an adolescent, particularly if the circumstances are unclear
- Torn, stained, or bloody underwear
- Bruising to the inner mouth or soft palate without a clear injury history

The presence of these signs does not confirm abuse, and the absence of these signs does not rule it out. A trained medical professional — ideally one with experience in child sexual abuse evaluations — is the appropriate person to assess and document physical findings. Many children's hospitals have specialized teams for exactly this purpose.

The Long Shadow: How Untreated Abuse Shows Up Later

Child sexual abuse does not end when the abuse stops. For many survivors, the effects of what happened to them in childhood ripple forward into adulthood in ways that can be disabling and isolating — and that often go unrecognized even by the survivors themselves as connected to their early experiences.

Adults who experienced childhood sexual abuse are significantly more likely to struggle with depression, anxiety, and post-traumatic stress disorder. They may have difficulty forming and maintaining healthy relationships, trusting other people, or feeling safe in intimate contexts. Many report feelings of shame and worthlessness that have followed them for decades. Substance abuse is common — alcohol and drugs become a way to manage memories and emotions that feel otherwise unmanageable.

Physical health consequences are also documented. Adults with childhood sexual abuse histories seek medical care at higher rates and report significantly higher rates of chronic pain, gastrointestinal problems, pelvic pain, and headaches. The connection between childhood trauma and adult physical health is well-established — and it underscores why treating child sexual abuse as the serious public health issue it is cannot wait.

Healing is possible. But it requires early intervention, consistent support, and adults who took the signs seriously when they first appeared.

None of this is inevitable. Children who receive early support — who are believed, who get appropriate therapy, who have at least one stable and loving adult consistently in their corner — are far more likely to heal and go on to live full, productive, connected lives. The signs this chapter describes are not just indicators of present suffering. They are opportunities — windows during which the right response from an adult can alter the entire trajectory of a child's life.

If you are reading this chapter and recognizing your child in what you see — stop here. Go to Chapter 7 now. It tells you exactly what to do, what to say, and what not to say. You do not need certainty. You do not need proof. You need to act on what you are seeing. Chapter 9 walks through the healing process in depth. But the most important thing you can do right now is take the next step — and Chapter 7 will walk you through it.

R E F E R E N C E S

1. Jenny, C., & Crawford-Jakubiak, J. E. (2013). The evaluation of children in the primary care setting when sexual abuse is suspected. Pediatrics, 132(2), e558–e567.

2. Child Welfare Information Gateway. (2023). Signs of Child Abuse. Retrieved from https://www.childwelfare.gov

3. RAINN. (2024). Effects of Sexual Violence. Retrieved from https://www.rainn.org/effects-sexual-violence

4. CDC. (2024). Preventing Child Sexual Abuse. Retrieved from https://www.cdc.gov/violenceprevention/childsexualabuse

5. Darkness to Light. (2023). Long-Term Effects of Child Sexual Abuse. Retrieved from https://www.d2l.org

Raising a Child Who Knows Their Worth

Education is protection. Not the one-time sex talk that everyone dreads and most children quickly forget — but an ongoing, age-appropriate, shame-free conversation that grows with your child from toddlerhood through adolescence. This chapter walks you through exactly what to say and when, organized by age, from the youngest children to teenagers. It also covers internet safety, dating, substances, and what your organization can do to reinforce these messages for every child in your care — not just the ones lucky enough to have parents doing this work at home.

Start With the Body: Names Matter

It starts with something as simple as what you call body parts. I know — it sounds small. But it is not. Every time a parent calls a vagina a "cookie" or a penis a "pee-pee," they are unintentionally sending a message that these parts are too embarrassing to name correctly, too shameful to speak about plainly. And children absorb that message. It becomes one more reason not to speak up when something happens.

> *A child who knows the correct name for their body parts is a child who can clearly report if something wrong happens to them.*

I know some parents who have gone their entire lives calling things 'the cookie' and 'the wee-wee.' I understand the impulse — those words feel softer, safer. But 'cookie' is not going to hold up in a forensic interview. Your child deserves the real words.

Using the correct anatomical names — penis, vagina, vulva, buttocks — from the very beginning does several important things. It normalizes the body. It gives children the precise language they need to communicate clearly if something happens to them. And it signals to them that you are the kind of adult they can talk to without shame. A child who goes to a teacher and says "Mr. Tom touched my cookie" may not be understood or taken seriously. A child who says "Mr. Tom touched my vagina" is unmistakably clear.

Start this at birth. You do not need to have a formal conversation about it — just use the correct words naturally during bath time, during diaper changes, during regular conversations about the body. By the time your child is old enough to need the words in a moment of crisis, they will already have them.

Body Autonomy: Teaching Children They Own Their Bodies

Body autonomy means that a child has the right to decide who touches their body and when. It sounds straightforward. In practice, we undermine it constantly without realizing it.

When we tell a child to hug Grandma even when they do not want to, we teach them that an adult's feelings are more important than the child's right to say no. When we tickle a child after they have asked us to stop, we teach them that a "no" from a child does not really count. These are small moments, and they come from a place of love and social expectation — but they plant the wrong seeds. A child who has been taught since toddlerhood that the adults around them get to override their bodily preferences is a much easier target for a grooming predator.

The fix is simple: give your child the option. Let them choose a high-five over a hug, a wave instead of a kiss. When a relative is offended, take that conversation to the adult privately — never at the expense of your child's boundary. Let your child see that you will back them up when they exercise their right to say no to physical contact they do not want.

> *Every time you honor your child's "no" about touch, you are teaching them that their body belongs to them. Predators count on children not knowing that.*

Extend the same principle to other aspects of physical contact. Ask permission before you touch a child who is upset. Respect it when they say they do not want to be touched right now. Model consent in the way you parent — and you will not need a special lecture about it. They will have learned it from watching you.

Age-by-Age Conversation Guide

The following conversation guide gives you the key messages to deliver at each developmental stage. These are not scripts — they are starting points. Use your own words, in your own voice, in the context of everyday moments. The goal is not a single talk. It is an ongoing, evolving dialogue that your child can return to at any time because they know the door is always open.

BABIES, TODDLERS & PRESCHOOLERS — AGES 0 TO 5

→ Use correct anatomical names for all body parts from birth

→ Teach that private parts are the areas a bathing suit covers

→ Your body belongs to you — no one should touch your private parts except a doctor when   Mommy or Daddy is in the room"

→ No one should ever ask you to keep a secret about your body

→ If anyone touches you in a way that feels wrong, tell me right away — you will not be in trouble

→ You do not have to hug or kiss anyone you do not want to

EARLY SCHOOL AGE — AGES 5 TO 8

→ Review all body safety rules from the previous stage, adding more detail

→ Safe touch vs. unsafe touch — explain the difference clearly with examples

→ Online safety: we do not talk to strangers online or share personal information

→ No adult should ever ask you to keep a secret from me — that is a body secret and it is not okay

→ If something happens and you are scared to tell me, tell any trusted adult — a teacher, a counselor, a coach

→ There is nothing you could ever tell me that would make me stop loving you

TWEENS — AGES 9 TO 12

→ Puberty education — what to expect and what is normal

→ Consent: your body belongs to you, and other people's bodies belong to them

→ Grooming: adults who are safe do not ask children to keep physical secrets

→ Digital safety: no nude photos — ever. Once a picture is sent, it cannot be taken back

→ If someone online makes you uncomfortable, stop talking to them and tell me immediately

→ Peer pressure and how to handle it — you do not have to do anything that feels wrong

→ I will always come get you, no questions asked, no matter where you are

<table>
<tr><td>

ADOLESCENTS — AGES 13 TO 17

→ Consent is enthusiastic, ongoing, and freely given — anything less is not consent

→ Healthy relationships: what they look like and the signs of an unhealthy one

→ Dating violence: it is not love if it feels like control, fear, or pressure

→ Sexting is a crime when it involves anyone under 18 — including you sending your own photos

→ Drugs and alcohol lower inhibitions and judgment — and predators know this

→ LGBTQ+ youth face higher rates of abuse — this conversation applies regardless of identity

→ If you are ever in a situation that feels dangerous, call me. I will not be angry. I will come get you.

</td></tr>
</table>

These conversations do not need to be formal sit-downs. They happen in the car. During bath time. At the dinner table. While watching the news. The best ones happen naturally, sparked by something you both just saw or heard. The goal is simply to keep talking — to establish yourself as the adult your child comes to when something goes wrong.

Internet and Digital Safety

Every chapter of this book has touched on digital safety because online risk is woven through every aspect of child sexual abuse in 2026. It deserves its own focused conversation with your child — one that is honest, specific, and repeated often.

Start with the basics and return to them regularly: do not share your real name, school, address, or

> *The most dangerous room in your house is wherever your child has an unsupervised device and no prior conversation about what to do when things go wrong.*

phone number with anyone online. Do not accept friend requests or follow requests from people you do not know in real life. If anyone online — regardless of how friendly they seem, regardless of whether they say they are a kid — asks you to do something that makes you uncomfortable, stop the conversation and come tell me immediately.

For older children and teenagers, get specific about sexting — the sending or receiving of sexually explicit images or messages. Explain that sending or receiving sexually explicit images of anyone under 18 — including themselves — can be charged as distribution of child sexual abuse material. This is not to frighten them into silence if something has already happened. It is to give them accurate information before it happens. If they have already received something they did not ask for, you want them to come to you — not delete it and say nothing, not forward it to a friend, but come to you.

> *Practical step: Review your child's privacy settings together. Turn off geotagging on photos. Set all social media accounts to private. Know which apps they are using and what those apps allow strangers to do. This is not surveillance — it is co-navigation. Do it together, not behind their back.*

The dangerous apps list changes constantly as new platforms emerge. Rather than trying to maintain a list of apps to avoid, focus on building the conversation and the relationship — a child who knows they can come to you without being punished is protected against every platform, not just the ones you happened to know about this week.

Safe Dating and Healthy Relationships

The dating conversation is one most parents approach too late and too awkwardly. By the time a teenager is already in a relationship — healthy or not — they have usually formed their baseline understanding of what relationships are supposed to feel like from their peers, from social media, and from whatever they absorbed watching the adults around them.

Start early. Long before your child is in a romantic relationship, talk about what healthy ones look like. Mutual respect. Honesty. The freedom to say no without consequences. The ability to spend time apart. A partner who celebrates your strengths rather than chipping away at your confidence. Make sure they know the warning signs of an unhealthy relationship: jealousy framed as love, isolation from friends and family, monitoring and controlling behavior, pressure to do things they are not comfortable with.

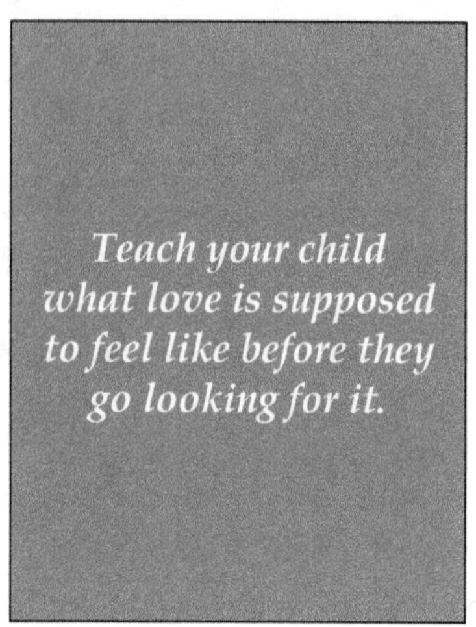

Have the conversation about consent with your sons explicitly and early — not just about the absence of no, but about the presence of yes. Affirmative consent means checking in with the person in front of you, continuously, not just once at the beginning. Do not assume they understand consent because no one has ever told them they do not. Boys need to hear, clearly and without embarrassment, that they do not have a right to someone else's body without ongoing, enthusiastic agreement — and that they need to model that standard in every relationship they enter. Ninety percent of sexual perpetrators are male. Most of them grew up in homes where no one ever had this conversation with them directly.

Have the same conversation with your daughters — not just about protecting themselves, but about their own responsibility to respect the boundaries of the people they are in relationship with. Every child, regardless of gender, needs to understand that consent is not a one-time checkbox. It is a continuous process of checking in with the person in front of you.

A Note to Organizations: Your Role in This Conversation

Not every child who walks through your doors has parents doing this work. Some children have no one at home having these conversations. Some are being abused by the very people who should be having them. For these children, you — the coach, the youth pastor, the school counselor, the camp director — may be the only adult in their life who is paying attention.

This does not mean your staff should be delivering sex education. It means your organization should create an environment where children feel safe, heard, and valued — where trusted adults are consistently present and consistently approachable. It means your staff know what the signs of abuse look like and are not afraid to ask a gentle question when something seems off. It means you have a clear, enforced reporting protocol so that when a child does say something, everyone knows exactly what to do next.

> *For some children, your organization is the only place where a trusted adult might notice, ask the right question, and change everything.*

Age-appropriate body safety education can be incorporated into your programming in a way that is simple, non-intrusive, and genuinely protective. Many evidence-based programs exist for churches, schools, sports programs, and camps — and they have been shown to reduce abuse and increase disclosure rates. Chapter 11 covers these programs in detail, along with the full organizational policy framework for keeping children safe in institutional settings.

R E F E R E N C E S

1. Darkness to Light. (2023). Body Safety Education. Retrieved from https://www.d2l.org

2. Stop It Now. (2024). Talking to Children About Sexual Abuse. Retrieved from https://www.stopitnow.org

3. Finkelhor, D. (2007). Prevention of Sexual Abuse Through Educational Programs Directed Toward Children. Pediatrics, 120(3), 640–645.

4. CDC. (2024). Prevention Strategies. Retrieved from https://www.cdc.gov/violenceprevention/childsexualabuse

5. RAINN. (2024). Talking to Your Kids About Sexual Assault. Retrieved from https://www.rainn.org/articles/talking-your-kids-about-sexual-assault

When a Child Speaks Up

The moment a child tells you they have been sexually abused is one of the most important moments of their life. Not because of what happened to them — though that matters enormously — but because of what happens next. This chapter covers everything you need to know about what to do — and what not to do — when a child comes to you. It covers disclosure, suspicion, discovery, reporting, and what happens after you make the call. None of this is easy. All of it is necessary.

Why Children Tell — and Why They Often Don't

Before we talk about how to respond, it helps to understand what it costs a child to speak up at all. By the time a child discloses, they have usually been carrying this alone for weeks, months, or sometimes years. They may have been told by their abuser that no one will believe them, that they will get in trouble, that telling will destroy their family. They may genuinely love the person who hurt them. They may feel responsible for what happened.

Children rarely tell the whole story the first time. They are testing to see if it is safe to tell you more.

Disclosure rarely happens in one clean conversation. Children typically disclose in fragments — testing the adult's reaction with a small piece before deciding whether it is safe to say more. They may say something and then immediately take it back. They may minimize what happened, or describe it in ways that seem vague or confusing. They may disclose to a peer before they disclose to a parent. They may not use the word "abuse" at all.

All of this is normal. It is not evasion — it is self-protection. A child who starts to tell and then stops has not changed their mind about what happened. They have decided, in that moment, that the risk of telling is too high. Every adult who works with children needs to understand this, because the way you respond to the first small disclosure determines whether you hear the rest of the story.

How to Respond When a Child Discloses

There is no perfect script for this moment. What matters most is not the exact words you use — it is the environment you create. A child who feels safe, believed, and not in trouble will keep talking. A child who senses panic, disbelief, or judgment will shut down.

Here is what that looks like in practice:

✔ WHAT TO DO	✖ WHAT NOT TO DO
→ Stay calm — your reaction is their permission to keep talking	→ Don't panic, cry, or express horror in front of the child
→ Listen more than you speak — let them tell it their way	→ Don't ask leading questions: "Did he touch your vagina?"
→ Say "I believe you" and mean it	→ Don't promise to keep it secret — you cannot and should not
→ Say "This is not your fault" clearly and directly	→ Don't interview repeatedly — involve trained professionals

→ Thank them for telling you — it took enormous courage	→ Don't express disbelief, even if the disclosure shocks you
→ Ask open questions only: "Can you tell me more?"	→ Don't ask why they didn't tell you sooner
→ Reassure them they are safe — tell them you will need to involve someone who can help	→ Don't confront the alleged abuser yourself
	→ Don't try to handle this alone without involving authorities

The most common mistake adults make is attempting to handle the disclosure themselves without involving authorities. This usually comes from a desire to protect the child from a difficult process, or from loyalty to the accused. Both are understandable impulses. Both ultimately harm the child. A disclosure handled privately, without professional involvement, almost always means the abuse continues.

> *You are not required to have all the answers in this moment. You are required to be calm, present, and to take the next right step — which is making sure a trained professional takes it from here.*

What a Child May Be Feeling After They Tell

Once a child has spoken, a complicated rush of emotion typically follows. They may feel immediate relief — the weight of the secret finally lifted. But that relief is often quickly followed by fear, regret, and guilt. They may worry about what will happen to the person who hurt them. They may feel they have broken something that cannot be fixed. They may be angry at you for your reaction, even if your reaction was appropriate.

The feelings that follow disclosure are often more overwhelming than the disclosure itself. Stay with the child through all of them.

Children frequently experience what researchers call "disclosure ambivalence" — the simultaneous desire for help and the desire to take back what they said. Do not be alarmed if a child recants shortly after disclosing. This does not mean they were lying. It almost always means they are frightened of the consequences. The original disclosure is almost always the truth.

Your job in the hours and days following a disclosure is not to keep discussing what happened — that is the job of trained investigators and therapists. Your job is to keep showing up. To maintain normalcy as much as possible. To reassure them, consistently and quietly, that they did the right thing, that you are not angry, and that you are not going anywhere.

When You Suspect Abuse but the Child Hasn't Said Anything

Sometimes a child does not tell you — but the signs are there. A change in behavior that cannot be explained. A physical symptom that does not add up. Something you witnessed, or something someone told you. Suspicion without disclosure is one of the most difficult positions an adult can find themselves in, and most people respond by doing nothing — telling themselves they might be wrong, that the accusation is too serious, that they will wait and see.

Waiting and seeing is not a neutral choice. Every day of delay is another day the abuse may continue. You do not need certainty to act — you need reasonable concern. Mandated reporters are required by law to report suspected abuse even without confirmation. Non-mandated reporters can and should do the same. The job of determining what happened belongs to trained investigators — your job is simply to make the call.

You do not need proof to report. You need reasonable concern. The investigation is not your job — reporting is.

If you suspect abuse, you can gently open the door without interrogating the child. A simple, calm question — "I've noticed you seem like you've been carrying something heavy lately. Is there anything you want to tell me?" — is not leading. It is not an interview. It is an invitation. And for some children, a single gentle invitation from the right adult at the right moment is all it takes.

How to Report: Steps and Resources

I know this part is a lot to absorb. I have sat with families trying to process CPS timelines and forensic interview protocols while their child was still not sleeping through the night. You do not need to understand the whole system today. You need to know the next step. That is it. One step at a time.

Once a child has disclosed or you have reasonable suspicion of abuse, reporting to the appropriate authorities is not optional — it is the necessary next step. Here is how to do it.

- Call your local Child Protective Services (CPS) or the police department in the jurisdiction where the abuse occurred. If you are unsure which agency to contact, the Childhelp National Child Abuse Hotline (1-800-422-4453) can guide you to the right agency in your state.

- You do not need to have all the information — provide what you know as clearly and specifically as possible. The name of the child, their age, the nature of the concern, the name of the alleged abuser if known, and how you became aware of the situation.

- If you are a mandated reporter — teacher, coach, medical provider, clergy, camp counselor, or other professional with regular contact with children — you are legally required to report. Failure to do so can result in criminal penalties.

- You do not need to tell the child's parents before you report, particularly if a parent may be the alleged abuser or if you believe notification could put the child at risk.

- Document what the child said to you as soon as possible after the conversation — in their words, not yours. Write down the date, time, and location of the disclosure. This documentation may be important for investigators.

NATIONAL RESOURCES — AVAILABLE 24 HOURS A DAY, 7 DAYS A WEEK

→ Childhelp National Child Abuse Hotline — 1-800-422-4453

→ RAINN National Sexual Assault Hotline — 1-800-656-HOPE (4673)

→ NCMEC CyberTipline — 1-800-843-5678

→ Darkness to Light Helpline — 1-866-FOR-LIGHT (367-5444)

→ Crisis Text Line — Text HOME to 741741

Mandated Reporters: Your Legal Obligation

In every U.S. state, certain professionals are legally designated as mandated reporters — meaning they are required by law to report known or suspected child abuse to the appropriate authorities. The list varies slightly by state but consistently includes:

- Teachers, school administrators, and other school personnel
- Physicians, physician assistants, nurse practitioners, and other healthcare providers
- Mental health professionals — psychologists, counselors, therapists, social workers
- Law enforcement officers
- Coaches, athletic directors, and youth sports staff
- Clergy and religious leaders (in most states)
- Childcare workers, camp counselors, and youth program staff
- Coroners and medical examiners

Mandatory reporters are required to report based on reasonable suspicion — not certainty, not proof, not a complete picture. The legal standard is deliberately low because the cost of failing to report is always higher than the cost of a report that is investigated and not substantiated. If you are a mandated reporter and you fail to report known or suspected abuse, you may face criminal penalties including fines and imprisonment. More importantly, you may be the last line of protection between a child and continued harm.

For organizational leaders: every person on your staff who has regular contact with children should know whether they are a mandated reporter in your state, what the reporting threshold is, and exactly what to do when that threshold is met. This is not optional training. It is the foundation of a child-safe organization. Chapter 11 includes a detailed framework for embedding mandatory reporting protocols into your organization's culture and procedures.

Taking Care of Yourself After a Disclosure

Receiving a disclosure of child sexual abuse is traumatic — full stop. This is true even for trained professionals who have heard these stories hundreds of times. If you are a parent, a teacher, a youth pastor — someone who loves this child — it is especially true. You may feel shock, rage, grief, helplessness, and guilt simultaneously. You may replay the conversation wondering if you said the right things. You may struggle to sleep. You may find yourself cycling between wanting to fix it and feeling utterly unable to.

> *You cannot pour from an empty cup. Taking care of yourself after a disclosure is not selfish — it is how you stay present for the child who needs you.*

All of this is a normal response to traumatic information. It does not mean you handled the disclosure badly. It means you are human, and you care about this child.

Find your own support — a trusted friend, a therapist, a support line. Talk to another adult about what you are experiencing. You cannot be fully present for a child who is healing if you are carrying this alone. And you should not have to.

REFERENCES

1. Darkness to Light. (2023). Responding to Disclosures of Child Sexual Abuse. Retrieved from https://www.d2l.org

2. RAINN. (2024). What to Do if a Child Discloses Sexual Abuse. Retrieved from https://www.rainn.org

3. Child Welfare Information Gateway. (2023). Mandatory Reporters of Child Abuse and Neglect. Retrieved from https://www.childwelfare.gov

4. Stop It Now. (2024). Help for Concerned Adults. Retrieved from https://www.stopitnow.org

5. London, K. et al. (2008). Review of the contemporary literature on how children report sexual abuse. Memory, 16(1), 29–47.

CHAPTER

8

Navigating the System

Knowing what to expect does not make this process easy. But it does make it survivable. And for a child who is watching the adults around them to gauge whether this was the right decision — whether telling was worth it — seeing you steady and informed makes an enormous difference.

What Happens After You Report

When a report of child sexual abuse is made to Child Protective Services (CPS) or law enforcement, a structured process begins immediately. Here is what that process typically looks like:

WHAT HAPPENS AFTER YOU REPORT

1. Intake screening — CPS reviews the report to determine if it meets the criteria for investigation. Cases that do not meet the threshold may be screened out; those that do are assigned to an investigator, typically within 24–72 hours.

2. Investigation begins — CPS and/or law enforcement conduct parallel investigations. They will interview the child, parents or caregivers, and other household members. Criminal records and prior CPS history are checked.

3. Child Advocacy Center (CAC) interview — In most jurisdictions, the child's forensic interview is conducted at a Child Advocacy Center by a trained specialist, in a child-friendly environment, to minimize the number of times the child must retell the story.

4. Medical evaluation — A medical examination is arranged, ideally within 72 hours if the abuse was recent. Trained providers document findings and collect forensic evidence if applicable.

5. Safety assessment — CPS evaluates whether the child is safe in their current environment. If imminent danger exists, the child may be temporarily removed or the alleged abuser may be asked to leave the home.

6. Case determination — After the investigation, CPS makes a finding: substantiated (abuse likely occurred), unsubstantiated (insufficient evidence), or unfounded. Substantiated cases may be referred for prosecution.

7. Services and support — Regardless of case outcome, CPS may offer counseling, parenting support, and other services to the family.

One of the hardest parts of this process for families is the loss of control. You made the report. You took the step. And now a series of strangers are making decisions about your child's life. That feeling is real and it is valid. What matters most in this phase is not managing the system — it is managing your presence. Stay calm in front of your child. Answer investigators' questions honestly. Do not coach your child on what to say. And find your own support so you can keep showing up.

> *You do not control the system. You control how you show up for your child while the system does its work.*

The Child Advocacy Center: A Gentler Path

If you have never heard of a Child Advocacy Center (CAC), you are not alone — but these organizations are one of the most important developments in child protection of the past three decades. Before CACs existed, a child who disclosed sexual abuse might be interviewed by a patrol officer, then a detective, then a CPS worker, then a prosecutor, then a medical provider — telling the same traumatic story over and over to strangers in clinical or intimidating settings. The research on what that does to a child is not good.

CACs bring all of the relevant professionals together in one place — law enforcement, CPS, medical providers, mental health professionals, and prosecutors — and conduct a single, coordinated forensic interview with the child. The interview is conducted by a specially trained forensic interviewer in a room designed to feel safe and non-threatening. Other team members observe via one-way mirror or video feed, eliminating the need for multiple interviews.

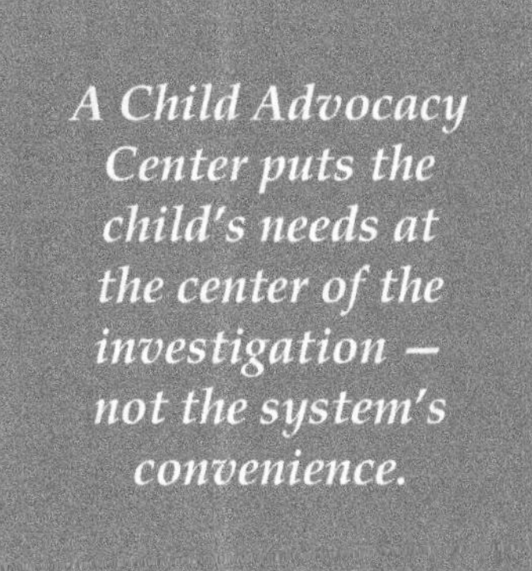

The CAC model has been shown to improve the quality of evidence collected, reduce trauma to child victims, and increase prosecution rates. As of 2024, there are more than 900 accredited CACs across the United States. To find the nearest one, visit the National Children's Alliance at www.nationalchildrensalliance. org.

> *If your child is referred for a forensic interview, prepare them by being honest: "Some people who help keep children safe want to talk with you. You can tell them exactly what happened. There are no right or wrong answers — just tell the truth." Do not rehearse, coach, or ask them to repeat what they said to you.*

The Medical Evaluation

A medical evaluation serves two purposes: it addresses the child's immediate physical health needs, and it collects evidence that may be used in prosecution. Both matter, and both are worth pursuing even if the abuse was not recent.

Medical evaluations for suspected child sexual abuse are ideally conducted by a physician, physician assistant, or nurse practitioner with specialized training in child abuse pediatrics, or by a Sexual Assault Nurse Examiner (SANE). These providers understand the sensitivity of the examination, know how to communicate with a child in a trauma-informed way, and are trained to document findings in a manner that is legally usable.

As covered in Chapter 5, the absence of physical findings does not mean abuse did not occur. The tissues of the genital and anal region heal quickly, often within days. A normal exam is documented and entered into the record — it neither confirms nor rules out abuse. What the exam does consistently find is evidence of the child's overall health, any sexually transmitted infections that require treatment, and in some cases physical findings that are consistent with abuse.

> *A normal physical exam does not mean abuse did not happen. Most child sexual abuse leaves no physical trace at all.*

Consent for the examination must be obtained — from the child's parent or guardian, and from the child themselves. A child always has the right to say no to any part of the exam at any time. If the child is resistant, do not force it. A delayed or partial exam is better than a traumatic one.

Understanding the Legal System

Child sexual abuse cases can involve two entirely separate legal systems — criminal and civil — and understanding the difference between them helps families make informed decisions about how to proceed.

CRIMINAL JUSTICE SYSTEM	CIVIL JUSTICE SYSTEM
→ State prosecutes the offender on behalf of society	→ Family controls the case and hires their own attorney
→ Standard of proof: beyond a reasonable doubt	→ Standard of proof: preponderance of evidence (more likely than not)
→ Child serves as a witness, not a party to the case	→ Family can sue for financial damages
→ Outcomes: probation, jail, prison, sex offender registration	→ A not-guilty verdict in criminal court does not bar a civil case
→ No financial cost to the family to prosecute	→ Legal fees are the family's responsibility (some attorneys work on contingency)
→ Prosecution timeline: 6 months to several years	→ Can hold institutions accountable — schools, churches, sports programs
→ Plea deals are common — charges may be reduced	→ Civil settlements may include confidentiality agreements

Most families will interact primarily with the criminal justice system, since that is where prosecution of the abuser takes place. But civil litigation is worth understanding — particularly for families whose child was abused within an institution. If a church, school, sports program, or youth organization failed in its duty to protect your child, a civil case may be the mechanism through which that institution is held accountable and required to change its practices.

What to Expect If the Case Goes to Court

The reality of child sexual abuse prosecution is that many cases never make it to trial. Charges may be reduced through plea bargaining. Cases may be dismissed for lack of evidence. Victims may recant under pressure. And even when cases do go to trial, the outcome is never guaranteed. This is painful. It is also the reality of a legal system that was not designed with child victims in mind, and that is slowly — too slowly — adapting.

If your case does proceed toward trial, here is what to expect. The child may be required to testify. Many jurisdictions now allow accommodations to reduce trauma — testimony via closed-circuit television, screens between the child and the defendant, support animals

> *The legal process is long, imperfect, and often deeply frustrating. It is also, for many families, the only path to accountability.*

or persons present during testimony. Ask the prosecutor what accommodations are available in your jurisdiction.

Trials take time. It is not unusual for a child sexual abuse case to take one to three years from report to verdict. During that period, the child and family will be periodically reminded of the abuse in ways that are emotionally difficult — subpoenas, depositions, pre-trial hearings. Consistent mental health support throughout this process is not optional. It is essential.

Whatever the outcome, the child's healing does not depend on a conviction. Children can and do recover from abuse regardless of whether the abuser is ever prosecuted. The legal process matters — accountability matters — but the child's recovery is built on the quality of support they receive, not on the verdict. Chapters 9 and 10 are devoted to exactly that.

How to Support Your Child Through the Process

While the system does its work, your child needs you to do yours. Here is what that looks like in practice:

- Be honest at a level appropriate to the child's age. They do not need to know every detail of the legal process, but they deserve truthful, age-appropriate answers to their questions. "I don't know" is always better than a reassuring lie that unravels later.

- Protect them from adult conversations about the case. Children should not overhear arguments between adults about the abuse, about the accused, or about what should happen next. These conversations belong behind closed doors.

- Maintain routine as much as possible. School, extracurriculars, mealtimes, bedtimes — the ordinary structure of daily life is grounding and stabilizing for a child in the middle of chaos.

- Let them take the lead on talking about it. Do not bring up the abuse unprompted. Be available, be open, and follow your child's cues. Some children want to talk often; others want to pretend nothing has changed. Both responses are normal.

- Connect them with a therapist who specializes in childhood trauma. This is the most important thing you can do. The sooner, the better. Chapter 9 covers how to find the right provider and what to expect from the healing process.

- Take care of yourself. Secondary trauma is real. A parent who is falling apart cannot hold a child together. Find your own therapist, your own support group, your own trusted person. You matter in this too.

R E F E R E N C E S

1. National Children's Alliance. (2024). Standards for Accredited Child Advocacy Centers. Retrieved from https://www.nationalchildrensalliance.org

2. Child Welfare Information Gateway. (2023). How the Child Welfare System Works. Retrieved from https://www.childwelfare.gov

3. RAINN. (2024). The Criminal Justice System. Retrieved from https://www.rainn.org/articles/criminal-justice-system

4. National Center for Victims of Crime. (2024). Child Sexual Abuse. Retrieved from https://victimsofcrime.org

5. Darkness to Light. (2023). After Disclosure: The Investigation Process. Retrieved from https://www.d2l.org

C H A P T E R

9

The Road to Healing

This chapter is for the families who are now on the other side of disclosure — past the report, past the initial crisis, and standing at the beginning of what is often the longest and most important stretch of the journey. It covers what healing actually looks like, what professional treatment is available and how to find it, how to support a child's recovery at home, and what parents and caregivers can do to take care of themselves in the process. Because this road is long, and you cannot walk it alone.

What Healing Actually Looks Like

One of the most important things a parent can understand about a child's healing process is that it is not linear. A child who seems to be doing well for weeks may suddenly regress — nightmares return, old behaviors reappear, anger surfaces from nowhere. This is not a setback. It is a normal part of how the brain and the body process trauma. Healing happens in waves, and the waves do not follow a predictable schedule.

> *Healing is not the absence of pain. It is the growing ability to carry that pain without being defined by it.*

Children also heal differently at different developmental stages. A child who was abused at age five and appears to have recovered may revisit the trauma in new ways at age twelve, when the meaning of what happened becomes clearer to them. A teenager who dissociated during abuse may not begin to process it until they feel safe enough to do so — sometimes years later. This is why ongoing support is important, not just crisis intervention at the point of disclosure.

What does healing look like when it is happening? It looks like a child who can talk about what happened without being consumed by it. A child who can name their feelings and ask for what they need. A child who begins to reinvest in the relationships and activities that bring them joy. A child who starts to see themselves as more than what was done to them. These markers do not appear on a schedule — but they do appear, with the right support, in the vast majority of children.

Getting Professional Help: Why Therapy Is Not Optional

I want to say this as directly as I can: therapy is the single most important thing you can do for a child who has experienced sexual abuse. Not the only thing — but the most important one. The love and support of family are essential and irreplaceable. They are not, by themselves, sufficient. Sexual abuse is a trauma that requires skilled, clinically proven professional treatment to process fully. Hoping a child will simply grow out of it, or that time will heal it on its own, is a risk no child should have to take.

> *Therapy is not a sign that something is permanently wrong with your child. It is the clearest sign that you are doing everything right.*

The good news is that the research on trauma treatment for children is strong. There are well-validated, highly effective approaches specifically designed for children who have experienced sexual abuse and other forms of trauma. The key is finding a therapist with the right training — someone who specializes in childhood trauma and uses evidence-based methods, not just a general therapist who is willing to try.

Evidence-Based Treatment Approaches

The approach with the strongest and most extensive research base for children who have experienced sexual abuse is Trauma-Focused Cognitive Behavioral Therapy — TF-CBT. When looking for a therapist, asking whether they are TF-CBT trained is the single most useful question you can ask.

TRAUMA-FOCUSED COGNITIVE BEHAVIORAL THERAPY (TF-CBT)

TF-CBT is the gold standard treatment for children who have experienced sexual abuse and other traumas. It is typically delivered over 12 to 25 sessions and involves both the child and a supportive caregiver. The child works with the therapist to process the trauma, develop coping skills, and reduce the distress associated with trauma memories. The caregiver component helps parents reinforce healing at home. TF-CBT is appropriate for children ages 3 to 18 and has strong evidence across diverse populations and backgrounds.

Other research-supported approaches include Child-Parent Psychotherapy (CPP) for children under age five, EMDR for children who struggle to verbalize their experiences, and trauma-informed play therapy for younger children who process best through play rather than talk. A qualified, trauma-trained therapist will know which approach fits your child's age, needs, and presentation — your job is to find that therapist, not to prescribe the method.

To find a TF-CBT trained therapist in your area, visit tfcbt.org. The National Child Traumatic Stress Network at nctsn.org also maintains a directory of trauma-informed providers and resources for families.

What to Look for in a Therapist

Finding the right therapist for a child who has experienced sexual abuse matters enormously. Not every licensed therapist has the training or experience to do this work effectively. Here is what to look for and what to ask:

- Specialized training in childhood trauma — ask specifically whether the therapist is trained in TF-CBT, CPP, EMDR, or another evidence-based trauma treatment. General licensure is not sufficient on its own.
- Experience working with children who have experienced sexual abuse — this population has specific needs that differ from other trauma presentations, and experience matters.
- A trauma-informed approach — the therapist should be able to explain how they think about trauma and how their approach addresses it specifically.
- Caregiver involvement — effective child trauma treatment almost always includes a parent or caregiver component. Be cautious of therapists who work exclusively with the child and do not involve the family.
- Good fit for your child — the therapeutic relationship matters. A child who does not feel safe with their therapist will not do the work. If your child is consistently resistant or distressed by sessions in ways that do not improve, it is worth considering whether the fit is right.

It is completely appropriate to interview a therapist before committing to treatment. Ask about their training, their approach, how they involve families, and what the treatment timeline typically looks like. A skilled, confident therapist will welcome these questions.

How to Support Your Child's Healing at Home

Therapy is where children do the focused work of processing trauma. Home is where that work is reinforced, grounded, and made real. The family environment — how safe it feels, how connected it is, how well it tolerates hard emotions — is the soil in which healing either takes root or does not. Here is what that looks like in practice:

- Believe them. Consistently, unwaveringly, and without qualification. A child who is believed heals differently from one who carries even the smallest seed of doubt about whether they were believed. Say it out loud, more than once, more than you think is necessary.
- Keep communication open. Do not force conversations about the abuse, but make clear that the door is always open. "You can talk to me about anything" is a message that needs to be repeated, not just said once.
- Validate their feelings without trying to fix them. When a child is angry, sad, or scared, the instinct is to reassure them that everything is fine. What they need more is to know that whatever they are feeling makes sense. "I understand why you feel that way" is more healing than "don't worry, it's okay."
- Maintain structure and routine. Predictability is safety for a traumatized child. Regular mealtimes, consistent bedtime routines, clear expectations — these are not rigid rules, they are anchors.
- Monitor for escalating symptoms. Watch for increasing withdrawal, self-harm, substance use, or expressions of hopelessness, and bring these to the therapist's attention promptly. Recovery is not always linear, and sometimes more intensive support is needed.
- Protect them from re-exposure. Court proceedings, family arguments about the case, news coverage, contact with the abuser — all of these can re-traumatize a child who is working to heal. Guard their environment deliberately.

A Word About Siblings and Other Children in the Home

When sexual abuse is disclosed within a family, the focus understandably goes to the child who was abused. But the siblings and other children in the home are also affected — sometimes significantly — and their needs can be overlooked in the initial crisis response.

Siblings may feel confused, guilty, or frightened. They may have witnessed things they did not understand, or they may be processing their own fear about whether they were also at risk. Older siblings sometimes feel they should have known and protected their brother or sister. Younger siblings may pick up on the emotional tenor of the household without understanding why things feel different.

Age-appropriate honesty with siblings goes a long way. They do not need the full details, but they deserve to know that something difficult happened and that it is being taken care of. Including siblings in family therapy sessions — when appropriate and when the treating therapist recommends it — can also help the whole family heal together rather than in isolated compartments.

Taking Care of Yourself: You Are Part of This Too

Secondary traumatic stress — sometimes called vicarious trauma — is a well-documented phenomenon in which the people closest to a trauma survivor develop their own trauma symptoms in response to what the survivor has experienced and shared. For parents of children who have been sexually abused, secondary traumatic stress is not a possibility. It is a near certainty.

You cannot be your child's safe harbor if you are drowning. Your healing matters — not just for you, but for them.

You may find yourself cycling between rage and grief. You may have intrusive thoughts about what was done to your child. You may struggle to sleep, to concentrate, to feel present in your own life. You may feel guilty for struggling, as if your pain is somehow a distraction from your child's. It is not. Your pain is real, it is valid, and it requires the same respect and care as your child's.

Find a therapist for yourself — ideally one who is familiar with trauma and the specific experience of non-offending parents of abuse survivors. There are also support groups specifically for parents in this situation; connecting with others who understand what you are going through can be profoundly relieving. RAINN, the Childhelp National Abuse Hotline, and local victim advocacy organizations can help you find these resources.

Your child is watching you. Not to see whether you are sad or angry — those responses are human and healthy. They are watching to see whether you are going to be okay. Whether the family is going to survive this. Whether life is still possible on the other side of what happened. The most powerful message you can send your child about their own resilience is the one you communicate by finding your own.

A Note to Organizations: When a Child in Your Care Is Healing

If a child in your program has experienced sexual abuse and is now in the process of healing, your organization has a continuing role to play — even after the report has been made and the professionals have taken over. That role is not clinical. It is relational. And it matters more than most organizational leaders realize.

A child who is working through trauma in therapy is still showing up at your school, your church, your sports program, your after-school center every week. The environment they encounter there — whether it feels safe, consistent, and free from the people or dynamics that caused harm — is either reinforcing their healing or working against it. Your staff do not need to be therapists to make a meaningful difference. They need to be informed, present, and steady.

Practically, this means a few things. First, communicate with the family — with appropriate boundaries and confidentiality — about how the organization can best support the child during this period. Ask whether there are specific triggers, accommodations, or adjustments that would help. Follow the family's lead, and follow the guidance of the treating therapist if they are willing to share it. Second, brief the staff members who work directly with the child — not with details of the abuse, but with enough context to respond appropriately if the child's behavior shifts or if they say something that warrants attention.

Secondary traumatic stress affects organizational staff too — particularly those who were close to the child or who were involved in the disclosure. Staff members who are struggling need access to support, whether through an employee assistance program, a debrief with leadership, or simply permission to acknowledge that what they witnessed was hard. An organization that takes care of its people in the aftermath of trauma builds the kind of culture where children are safe in the first place.

Finally, if the abuse occurred within your organization — if the offender was a staff member, volunteer, or someone operating under your supervision — the healing process carries an additional layer of institutional accountability. Families in that situation need to see the organization take concrete, visible action: removing the offender, reviewing policies, communicating transparently with the broader community where appropriate, and committing to the structural changes that prevent recurrence. Chapter 11 covers that framework in full. But the starting point is the same as it is for everyone on this road: show up, stay present, and do not look away.

R E F E R E N C E S

1. Cohen, J. A., Mannarino, A. P., & Deblinger, E. (2017). Treating Trauma and Traumatic Grief in Children and Adolescents (2nd ed.). Guilford Press.

2. National Child Traumatic Stress Network. (2024). About Child Trauma. Retrieved from https://www.nctsn.org

3. RAINN. (2024). Recovery from Sexual Violence. Retrieved from https://www.rainn.org/articles/recovery-sexual-violence

4.   TF-CBT Web. (2024). Trauma-Focused CBT for Children and Adolescents. Retrieved from https://tfcbt.org

5.   Darkness to Light. (2023). Healing Resources for Families. Retrieved from https://www.d2l.org

CHAPTER

10

Beyond Surviving

This chapter looks further down the road than most of this book. If you are in the early weeks or months after a disclosure, some of what follows may feel distant right now. That is okay. Read it anyway — because knowing where the road goes makes the early miles easier to walk. This chapter is for survivors who are further along, for the adults who love them, and for anyone who needs to know that the destination is real.

From Surviving to Thriving: What the Research Shows

There is actual research on this — not just hope, not just anecdote, but documented science. Psychologists Richard Tedeschi and Lawrence Calhoun spent decades studying what happens to people after serious trauma and found something that surprised a lot of people: many survivors report meaningful positive changes that came directly from wrestling with what happened to them. They called it post-traumatic growth. It shows up as deeper relationships, a clearer sense of what matters, a stronger sense of personal strength, and — for many people — a feeling that their life has more purpose than it did before.

> *Trauma does not have to be the loudest thing about a person. With the right support, it becomes one chapter — not the whole story.*

That does not mean the trauma was good. It does not mean survivors should be grateful for it. It means human beings are more resilient than we give them credit for, and that suffering and growth can coexist in the same person at the same time. Knowing that is possible matters — especially when you are still in the middle of the hard part and cannot yet see where it leads.

For child sexual abuse survivors specifically, the research on long-term outcomes is more hopeful than most people realize. Survivors who were believed, who got appropriate support and treatment, who had at least one stable and loving adult in their corner — these survivors show significantly better outcomes across every measure: mental health, physical health, relationships, work, life satisfaction. Here is the most important finding: the variables that predict poor outcomes are not the abuse itself. They are the absence of support in its aftermath. That is the variable families and organizations can change. That is the whole point of this book.

Reclaiming Identity: You Are More Than What Happened to You

One of the quietest and most lasting effects of childhood sexual abuse is what it does to how a child sees themselves. Abuse sends a message — not in words, but in the most visceral way possible — that the child's body is not their own, that their no does not count, that they exist for someone else's use. Children absorb that message. Most do, to some degree, without anyone ever knowing it is happening. They grow up feeling somehow different from everyone else. Damaged. Like there is a version of them that was lost and cannot be recovered.

The work of reclaiming identity is hard. There is no shortcut around it. It means learning to separate yourself from what happened to you

What happened to you is part of your story. It is not your identity. You get to decide what the rest of the chapters say.

— understanding that it was done to you, it was not caused by you, and it is not who you are. It means rebuilding a relationship with your own body — one based on ownership and safety rather than violation. And it means writing a bigger story. One where you are the author, not a character that other people act upon.

This work is best done in therapy, with someone who understands trauma and how it reshapes identity. But it also happens in small everyday moments — every time a survivor sets a boundary that holds, or lets someone truly know them, or chooses to describe themselves by something other than what happened. Those moments add up. They are the work.

Relationships After Abuse: Trust, Intimacy, and Healing

Childhood sexual abuse is almost always perpetrated by someone the child trusted. That fact — that the harm came from someone who was supposed to be safe — leaves a particular kind of damage to a survivor's ability to trust other people. It is not irrational. It is a learned response to a real experience. The problem is that it does not stay contained to the person who caused it. It bleeds into other relationships — partners, friends, family, anyone in a position of authority — often without the survivor fully understanding why.

Some survivors respond by keeping everyone at arm's length — better to push people away than risk being hurt again. Others move in the opposite direction, attaching quickly and intensely to anyone who offers warmth, sometimes to people who are not safe. Both patterns come from the same wound. Both are worth understanding in therapy, where a skilled provider can help a survivor recognize the pattern, understand where it came from, and begin to change it.

> *Learning to trust again is not about forgetting what happened. It is about building the evidence, one relationship at a time, that safety is possible.*

Intimate relationships can be especially difficult. Triggers, dissociation, fear that has nothing to do with the current partner and everything to do with the past — these are common and they are not character flaws. They are the body remembering. This is one of the areas where open communication with a partner and support from a trauma-informed therapist can make the most difference. Many survivors build deeply loving, fully intimate partnerships. It takes time, honesty, and patience — and it is possible.

For parents and family members: if your child is now an adolescent or young adult navigating relationships after abuse, the most powerful thing you can offer is a relationship with you that shows them what safe connection looks like. Stay in their life. Be consistent. Do not require them to be okay before you show up.

When the Hard Seasons Come Back

Long-term survivors of childhood sexual abuse often describe the healing process in terms of seasons — long periods of relative peace and stability, punctuated by harder stretches when something brings the past back to the surface. These seasons are not failures. They are not signs that previous healing did not take. They are the way trauma works in a human life.

Common triggers for these harder seasons include: entering a new intimate relationship, becoming a parent, having a child reach the age at which the abuse began, a news story or cultural moment that resonates with personal experience, the death of the abuser, a legal proceeding, or simply a milestone birthday that prompts reflection on the life lived so far. Any of these can bring material to the surface that felt resolved — and finding that it is still tender does not mean the survivor is back at square one.

> *For survivors navigating a difficult season: returning to therapy — even briefly — is not a sign of failure. It is a sign of self-awareness and self-care. Many survivors find that shorter, focused courses of therapy at key life transitions are more helpful than a single long stretch of treatment earlier in life.*

For the people who love a survivor: when a hard season comes, your instinct may be to fix it or to panic. Neither helps. What helps is the same thing that has always helped — showing up, staying present, and making clear through your actions that you are not going anywhere. The survivor in your life already knows the hard things. What they may not yet fully know is that they are worth staying for. Keep proving that they are.

Turning Pain Into Purpose: The Power of Advocacy

For many survivors, one of the most meaningful aspects of the healing journey is the discovery that their experience — the hardest thing they have ever carried — can be used to protect other children. Advocacy, in whatever form it takes, is one of the most consistently documented pathways to post-traumatic growth in the survivor literature. It transforms the survivor's relationship to their own story: from something that was done to them, to something they are doing something about.

> *Some of the most powerful child protection advocates in the world are survivors. Not despite what happened to them — because of what they chose to do with it.*

Advocacy does not have to look like public speaking or organizational leadership, though for some survivors it does. It can look like being the parent who has the uncomfortable conversation with their child's school. The family member who insists on background checks for youth volunteers at their church. The coach who creates a culture where kids feel safe to speak up. The survivor who tells their story to one other person who needed to hear it. Every form of advocacy counts. Every child protected is the whole point.

If you are a survivor reading this and you feel called toward advocacy, know that there is a community waiting for you. Organizations like RAINN, Darkness to Light, and the National

Center for Victims of Crime all have volunteer and advocacy programs. The Crusader for Kids movement — the foundation behind this book — exists precisely to create a network of informed, equipped, passionate advocates who refuse to look away. Your experience is not a disqualifier. It is your credential.

A Letter to Survivors

I want to speak directly to you for a moment — if you are a survivor reading this book, whether you are doing so because you are a parent trying to protect your own children, a professional trying to do your job better, or simply someone who is still finding their way through.

What happened to you was not your fault. Not any part of it. Not because of what you were wearing or where you were or how old you were or how you responded in the moment. Not because you did not fight back, or because you did not tell sooner, or because there were moments when it felt like something other than what it was. None of that is on you. The full weight of what happened belongs to the person who chose to do it.

You have survived something that would have broken many people. The fact that you are still here — still reading, still trying, still building a life — matters. It is not a small thing. And wherever you are on this road, whether you feel like you are thriving or still just barely holding on, you are not behind. There is no schedule. There is no finish line you are supposed to have crossed by now. There is only the next right step, and the one after that.

You are allowed to heal. You are allowed to be happy. You are allowed to have relationships that feel safe and a life that feels full and a future that is not defined by your past. None of those things are luxuries reserved for people who had easier childhoods. They are yours. And the work of claiming them — as hard as it is, as long as it takes — is some of the most courageous work a human being can do.

Keep going.

REFERENCES

1. Tedeschi, R. G., & Calhoun, L. G. (2004). Post-traumatic Growth: Conceptual Foundations and Empirical Evidence. Psychological Inquiry, 15(1), 1–18.

2. RAINN. (2024). Recovery from Sexual Violence. Retrieved from https://www.rainn.org/articles/recovery-sexual-violence

3. National Center for Victims of Crime. (2024). Healing from Sexual Assault. Retrieved from https://victimsofcrime.org

4. Darkness to Light. (2023). Survivor Resources. Retrieved from https://www.d2l.org

5. van der Kolk, B. (2014). The Body Keeps the Score: Brain, Mind, and Body in the Healing of Trauma. Viking.

Building a Village — A Practical Guide for Organizations That Serve Children

If you are reading this as a leader of an organization that serves children — a pastor, a principal, a coach, a camp director, a youth program coordinator — this chapter is written directly to you.

If you picked up this book and flipped straight to this chapter — good. That is exactly the kind of leadership this work needs.

This chapter is for the builders. The organizational leaders, the ministry directors, the coaches, the school administrators, the youth program coordinators who have read this far and are now asking the most important question: what do I actually do with all of this? The answer is not one thing. It is a series of deliberate decisions — about policies, about training, about culture, about accountability — that together create an environment where children are protected and where abuse, if it occurs, is reported and addressed rather than hidden.

None of this requires a massive budget or a full-time compliance officer. It requires leadership that takes child safety seriously — not as a liability concern, but as a mission commitment. And it requires the willingness to look honestly at where your organization currently stands and do the work of getting better.

Why Organizations Are on the Front Line

Every organization that serves children is, by definition, a place where adults have regular, structured access to children in their care. That is a gift — it is exactly the environment in which trusted adults can make a profound positive difference in a child's life. It is also, without proper safeguards, an environment that predators actively seek out and exploit.

The research on where child sexual abuse occurs is clear. Most abuse does not happen in dark alleys or in strangers' cars. It happens in exactly the kinds of settings we are talking about — churches, schools, sports programs, youth organizations, camps. It happens where adults have earned trust, where children are regularly present, and where institutional culture has allowed concerning behavior to go unchallenged for too long.

This is not an indictment of organizations that serve children — it is a call to them. The same trust and access that makes your program valuable to children is what makes your commitment to safety non-negotiable. You do not get to serve children well without also protecting them well. Those two things are not separate missions. They are the same mission.

The Foundation: Screening and Hiring

The most effective child protection policy in the world cannot compensate for putting the wrong person in the room with a child. Screening is the first line of defense, and it is one that too many organizations treat as a formality rather than a serious protective measure.

Here is what a genuine screening process looks like — not the checkbox version, but the real one:

SCREENING STANDARDS: ANYONE WORKING WITH CHILDREN

1. Criminal background check

2. Sex offender registry check

3. Reference checks

4. Written application with behavioral questions

5. In-person interview

6. Ongoing periodic re-screening

Important: A clean background check does not mean a person is safe. Most abusers have no prior criminal record. Screening reduces risk — culture and supervision do the rest.

The Policies That Actually Protect Children

Policies are only as good as the culture that enforces them. But the right policies, consistently applied, change behavior — and changed behavior changes outcomes. Here are the policies that child safety experts identify as most essential:

- Two-adult rule — no adult should ever be alone with a child in an unsupervised, private setting. This applies to staff and volunteers without exception. This single policy eliminates the primary condition predators require to operate.
- Open-door rule — one-on-one interactions between adults and children should take place in visible, observable spaces. Closed doors with children inside should be treated as a policy violation, not a minor oversight.
- Appropriate touch policy — define clearly what physical contact is and is not appropriate in your setting. Post it. Train to it. Enforce it consistently.
- Digital communication policy — all communication between staff or volunteers and children should go through official channels where parents can see it, or with a parent

copied. Private messaging, social media contact, and texting between adults and minors in your program should be prohibited.

- Overnight and off-site policy — any overnight programming involving children requires enhanced supervision ratios, clear sleeping arrangements that preserve appropriate boundaries, and explicit policies about adult access to children's sleeping areas.
- Mandatory reporting policy — every staff member and volunteer should know your organization's reporting chain and their own legal obligations as mandated reporters. Post the reporting hotline numbers. Practice the process before it is needed.
- Response and removal policy — if a concern about a staff member or volunteer is raised, there must be a clear, immediate protocol: removal from contact with children pending investigation, no internal investigation in place of law enforcement reporting, and no return to program until the concern is fully resolved.

Write these policies down. Put them in your staff handbook, your volunteer orientation materials, and your parent communications. A policy that exists only in someone's head is not a policy — it is a hope.

Training: Your Policies Are Only as Strong as Your People

Every person in your organization who has regular contact with children needs training — not a one-time orientation, but recurring, substantive education on child safety. This includes paid staff, volunteers, board members, and leadership. No one in a child-serving organization gets a pass on this.

> *A policy on paper protects no one. The training that makes it real is what protects children.*

What should that training cover? At minimum: what child sexual abuse is and how it happens, the grooming process and the warning signs in adults and children, your organization's specific policies and why each one exists, how to respond when a child discloses, and your mandatory reporting obligations and process. This book covers all of it — and it is a strong foundation for organizational training conversations.

For organizations that want a structured program to take their team through this content, the Safe Talk Prevention Program — developed through Crusader for Kids — is a preventative education and awareness program designed specifically for organizational settings. It equips staff and volunteers with the knowledge to recognize the signs of child sexual abuse, understand how grooming works, respond appropriately when a child discloses, and create a culture where children are safer from the start. The Safe Talk Prevention Program is built for churches, schools, sports programs, youth organizations, camps, and any setting where adults serve children. To learn more or to bring it to your organization, visit www.tiffanysjohnson.com.

Additional nationally recognized resources and programs for child-serving organizations are listed in the appendix at the back of this book.

Culture: The Thing Policies Cannot Create Alone

Here is something I have come to believe firmly: the organizations that most effectively protect children are not necessarily the ones with the most comprehensive policy manuals. They are the ones where the culture makes it safe for anyone — a child, a parent, a junior staff member — to say something when something feels wrong.

Culture is what happens when no one is watching. Build a culture where protecting children happens even then.

That kind of culture does not happen by accident. It is built deliberately, over time, through the messages leadership sends — in what they celebrate, what they tolerate, and what they refuse to ignore. When a leader shrugs off a boundary violation because the person in question is beloved and valuable to the program, they send a message to everyone watching: status protects you here. When a leader addresses the same violation directly and consistently regardless of who committed it, they send a different message entirely: no one is above the safety of the children in our care.

Build a culture where children are seen as people with rights, not just recipients of your program's services. Teach the children in your care about body safety in age-appropriate ways — not in a way that frightens them, but in a way that gives them language and permission to name what does not feel right. Create multiple reporting pathways so that a child or adult who is uncomfortable going to a particular leader has someone else they can go to. And make sure that when someone does report a concern, they are thanked for it — not made to feel that they have caused a problem.

When Something Happens: Responding Well

Every organization that serves children long enough will face this moment — a disclosure, a concern, an allegation. How you respond in that moment says everything about whether your commitment to child safety is real or just rhetorical.

The response that protects children and the organization's integrity looks like this: the child is believed and supported immediately. The alleged offender is removed from contact with children immediately — not after an internal investigation, not after a conversation with the accused, immediately. Law enforcement and child protective services are contacted the same day. The organization's leadership does not attempt to handle this internally or to protect its reputation at the expense of the child. Transparency, within appropriate legal and confidentiality boundaries, is the standard — not concealment.

The organizations that have suffered the most catastrophic reputational and legal consequences from child sexual abuse are, almost without exception, the ones that chose concealment over accountability. The Catholic Church. Penn State. USA Gymnastics. The Boy Scouts. The pattern is always the same: a trusted adult abuses children, leadership is informed or has reason to suspect, and the institutional response is to manage the situation rather than report it. Every time, it makes things worse. Every time, more children are harmed. Every time, the reckoning is more severe than it would have been had the truth been told immediately.

> *Concealment is not protection. Every organization that has tried to handle abuse internally has made it worse — for the child, for the survivors who came before, and for the institution itself.*

Your organization does not have to be in that story. The path away from it is not complicated. It is just hard. Report. Remove. Support the child. Change the conditions that allowed it to happen. And do it even when it is costly — because the alternative is always more costly.

Body Safety Education in Your Programming

One of the most powerful things an organization can do — and one of the least utilized — is build age-appropriate body safety education directly into its programming. Not as a one-time special session, but as an ongoing, normalized part of what it means to be a child in your community.

Research consistently shows that children who receive body safety education are more likely to recognize and report abuse, and that this education does not traumatize or alarm children when it is delivered in an age-appropriate, matter-of-fact way. The fear that talking to children about body safety will frighten them or rob them of innocence is understandable — and it is not supported by the evidence. What robs children of innocence is abuse. Education protects it.

Chapter 6 covers the age-by-age conversation framework in detail. For organizations, the application is straightforward: build these conversations into your curriculum, your youth group, your classroom, your team culture. Partner with parents so families are reinforcing the same messages at home. And make sure the adults in your organization have had the training to deliver these conversations confidently and consistently.

A Final Word: This Is the Work

I started Crusader for Kids because I believe that most of the child sexual abuse that happens in this country is preventable. Not all of it — there will always be predators who find ways around the safeguards. But the majority of it happens because adults were not informed enough to recognize the signs, or institutions were not equipped to respond, or children were not empowered to tell. Those are all fixable problems.

This book is one tool. The training programs referenced in this chapter are more tools. Your organization's policies and culture are the infrastructure. And the adults in your community — parents, coaches, teachers, pastors, neighbors, volunteers — are the village. Every single one of them who reads this book, takes this training, has this conversation, or changes one practice in their program is a child protected who might not have been.

That is not a small thing. That is the whole thing.

The children in your care are worth everything this requires. They are counting on you — not because they know your name or your title, but because they are in your program, in your school, in your church, on your team. They are there. You are there. That is enough of a reason.

Build the village. Protect the children. Do the work.

R E F E R E N C E S

1. Crusader for Kids. (2024). Safe Talk Prevention Program. Retrieved from https://www.tiffanysjohnson.com

2. Stop It Now. (2024). Creating Safe Organizations. Retrieved from https://www.stopitnow.org

3. Child Welfare Information Gateway. (2023). Preventing Child Abuse and Neglect. Retrieved from https://www.childwelfare.gov

4. Finkelhor, D., et al. (2015). Improving the Response of Child Protective Services to Child Sexual Abuse. Child Abuse & Neglect, 46, 24–35.

5. National Center for Missing and Exploited Children. (2024). Resources for Organizations. Retrieved from https://www.missingkids.org

Myths & Facts

Myths and Facts About Child Sexual Abuse

The following myths are among the most common — and most dangerous — misconceptions about child sexual abuse. Each one creates gaps in awareness that abusers exploit. Understanding what is true is the first step toward building communities where children are safer.

1. **MYTH:** Child sexual abuse is rare.

   FACT: It is far more common than most people realize. According to the CDC, approximately 1 in 4 girls and 1 in 13 boys in the United States experience sexual abuse at some point in childhood. Most cases are never reported.

2. **MYTH:** Child sexual abuse is committed by strangers.

   FACT: In the overwhelming majority of cases — more than 90% — the abuser is someone the child knows and trusts. This includes family members, family friends, coaches, teachers, clergy, and neighbors.

3. **MYTH:** Child sexual abuse (CSA) only occurs in poor, uneducated communities.

   FACT: Child sexual abuse occurs across all demographics regardless of income, education, race, or religion. While poverty can increase certain risk factors, no community is immune. Abuse happens in wealthy, educated, and faith-based communities just as it does everywhere else.

---

4. **MYTH:** Sex trafficking and child exploitation only happen overseas or in big cities.

   FACT: Child sex trafficking happens in every state, in suburbs and rural communities as well as cities. The National Center for Missing and Exploited Children received over 32 million reports to its Cyber Tip line in 2023 alone. The average age of entry into commercial sexual exploitation is between 12 and 14 years old.

---

5. **MYTH:** Children who are sexually abused will always show physical signs.

   FACT: Most child sexual abuse leaves no visible physical evidence. Many forms of abuse — including non-contact abuse, grooming, and certain types of touching — do not cause physical injury. Behavioral and emotional changes are often the only indicators.

---

6. **MYTH:** Children make up stories about being sexually abused.

   FACT: Research consistently shows that false reports of child sexual abuse are rare. Children are far more likely to minimize or delay disclosing abuse than to fabricate it. When a child does speak up, they should always be believed and reported to appropriate authorities.

---

7. **MYTH:** If a child doesn't fight back or say no, it wasn't really abuse.

   FACT: Children rarely fight back. Fear, confusion, loyalty to the abuser, threats, and the grooming process all suppress resistance. Compliance or silence does not equal consent. Children cannot legally consent to sexual activity with adults, period.

---

8. **MYTH:** Only girls are victims of child sexual abuse.

   FACT: Boys are abused at significant rates — approximately 1 in 13 — but are far less likely to report. Social stigma, shame, and fear that they will not be believed prevent many male victims from disclosing. Boys deserve the same belief, support, and access to care as girls.

9. **MYTH:** Children who are sexually abused will inevitably go on to abuse others.

   FACT: This is one of the most harmful myths, as it stigmatizes survivors. The vast majority of survivors never perpetrate abuse. With appropriate support, therapy, and intervention, children who have experienced abuse can heal and lead healthy lives.

10. **MYTH:** Sexual abuse by a family member is less harmful than abuse by a stranger.

    FACT: Abuse by a trusted family member often causes deeper and longer-lasting psychological harm because it violates the child's primary relationship of safety. Betrayal trauma — the damage caused when someone the child depends on causes harm — can be among the most difficult to heal.

Sources: CDC, RAINN, NCMEC, Darkness to Light (2024–2026)

Additional Resources for Organizations

The organizations and programs listed below are nationally recognized resources for child-serving organizations working to prevent child sexual abuse. They are offered here as supplementary tools — not as replacements for your organization's own policies, training culture, or engagement with the Safe Talk Prevention Program. Each has been vetted for credibility and practical usefulness.

Prevention Training Programs

DARKNESS TO LIGHT — STEWARDS OF CHILDREN

→ A widely used prevention training program for adults who work with children

→ Available online and in-person — approximately two hours to complete

→ Covers recognizing, reacting to, and reporting child sexual abuse

→ Visit: www.d2l.org

PRAESIDIUM

→ Provides organizational risk assessment, training tools, and consulting for child-serving organizations

→ Specializes in abuse risk management for youth-serving nonprofits

→ Visit: www.praesidiuminc.com

DARKNESS TO LIGHT — 5 STEPS TO PROTECTING OUR CHILDREN

→ A free online awareness training designed for any adult — not just professionals

→ Covers the five key steps adults can take to reduce child sexual abuse

→ Visit: www.d2l.org/education/5-steps

Reporting and Crisis Resources

CHILDHELP NATIONAL CHILD ABUSE HOTLINE

→ Available 24 hours a day, 7 days a week

→ Provides crisis intervention, information, and referrals to local services

→ Phone: 1-800-422-4453 | Visit: www.childhelp.org

RAINN — RAPE, ABUSE & INCEST NATIONAL NETWORK

→ Operates the National Sexual Assault Hotline in partnership with local rape crisis centers

→ Provides resources for survivors, families, and organizations

→ Phone: 1-800-656-HOPE (4673) | Visit: www.rainn.org

NATIONAL CENTER FOR MISSING AND EXPLOITED CHILDREN (NCMEC)

→ Operates the CyberTipline for reporting online child sexual exploitation

→ Provides free training and resources for youth-serving organizations

→ Phone: 1-800-843-5678 | Visit: www.missingkids.org

Policy Frameworks and Organizational Standards

STOP IT NOW!

→ Provides resources for organizations on creating safe environments for children

→ Includes guidance on policies, training, and responding to concerning behavior

→ Visit: www.stopitnow.org

CHILD WELFARE INFORMATION GATEWAY

→ A service of the U.S. Children's Bureau providing resources on child abuse prevention

→ Includes state-by-state information on mandatory reporting laws and statutes

→ Visit: www.childwelfare.gov

NATIONAL CHILDREN'S ALLIANCE — CHILD ADVOCACY CENTERS

→ Accredits Child Advocacy Centers nationwide

→ Directory of local CACs available for organizations seeking referral partners

→ Visit: www.nationalchildrensalliance.org

For information about the Safe Talk Prevention Program and Crusader for Kids resources, visit www.tiffanysjohnson.com.

A P P E N D I X   B

Understanding Offender Profiles

This appendix is referenced from Chapter 4. It provides a more detailed look at the behavioral categories researchers have identified among child sexual offenders. These profiles are tools for understanding patterns — not diagnostic labels, and not a substitute for professional assessment. No offender fits neatly into a single category, and the same person may exhibit traits from more than one profile at different times or with different victims. What matters for protective purposes is not the label — it is recognizing the behavior.

A clean background check does not mean a person fits none of these profiles. Most child sexual abusers — particularly preferential offenders — have no prior criminal record when they first come into contact with a child-serving organization. These profiles are most useful not for screening out known offenders, but for helping adults recognize patterns of behavior that warrant closer attention.

THE SITUATIONAL OFFENDER

The situational offender does not have a primary sexual attraction to children. They typically have adult relationships and may appear to be functioning well in their personal and professional life. Abuse occurs as a result of circumstance — stress, opportunity, impulsivity, or the presence of a vulnerable child at a moment of significant personal weakness. Substance abuse is frequently a contributing factor. Incest offenders are often placed in this category. Because they do not fit the public image of a predator, situational offenders are frequently the last person anyone suspects. Their abuse is often discovered only after a disclosure — rarely through behavioral observation beforehand.

THE PREFERENTIAL OFFENDER

The preferential offender has a genuine, primary sexual attraction to children. They seek out children deliberately, invest significant time and effort in gaining access to them, and may have been doing so for years — sometimes decades — before anyone notices. They frequently pursue careers or volunteer roles that place them in regular, trusted contact with children: coaching, teaching, youth ministry, scouting, childcare. Their warmth toward children feels genuine to the adults around them, which is precisely what makes them so dangerous and so difficult to identify. This type tends to have multiple victims across extended periods of time, and their grooming behavior is calculated and patient.

THE OPPORTUNISTIC OFFENDER

The opportunistic offender acts on impulse when a situation presents itself, without the deliberate premeditation of the preferential type. They may not have a persistent or primary attraction to children, but will exploit access and vulnerability when the conditions are right — typically when supervision is absent and a child is isolated. This is the offender type most directly addressed by structural safeguards: two-adult policies, open-door rules, and clear supervision standards eliminate the conditions opportunistic offenders require. Reducing opportunity is the most effective defense against this profile.

THE COERCIVE OR SADISTIC OFFENDER

The coercive or sadistic offender is the rarest type and the most dangerous. This offender is motivated primarily by power and control rather than by affection or sexual attraction, and the suffering of the victim may itself be part of the gratification. They are significantly more likely to use physical force, threats, or abduction than other offender types. The cases that make national headlines — stranger abductions, violent assaults on children — typically involve this profile. While rare in comparison to the other types, awareness of this category is important for educating children about physical safety in public spaces and for understanding the full spectrum of risk.

A Word to Those Who Are Struggling

If you are someone who is experiencing sexual thoughts or urges toward children — and you have not acted on them — this section is for you. What you are reading takes courage. The fact that you are here, reading a book about protecting children, may mean you are already looking for a way out of something that frightens you. That matters.

Sexual attraction to children is a condition that some people did not choose and do not want. Acting on it, however, is a choice — one with devastating and irreversible consequences for the child, and life-altering consequences for you. The research on treatment for people who struggle with this is clear: help is available, treatment works, and reaching out before anything happens is the most important step you can take.

If you have already acted on these urges and a child has been harmed, the most important thing you can do right now is stop, get help, and do not allow another child to be hurt. The path forward is hard. It is not impossible.

You do not have to figure this out alone. The organizations below provide confidential support, treatment referrals, and helplines specifically for people who are concerned about their own thoughts or behaviors toward children. Making this call — before a child is hurt — is the most protective thing you can do.

RESOURCES FOR THOSE SEEKING HELP

→ **Stop It Now! Helpline — 1-888-PREVENT (773-8368) | www.stopitnow.org**

→ **Association for the Treatment of Sexual Abusers (ATSA) — www.atsa.com/referral**

→ **Child Molestation Research and Prevention Institute — www.childmolestationprevention.org**

REFERENCE

1.   Ramsland, K. & McGrain, P. (2010). Inside the Minds of Sexual Predators. Praeger.

PRAISE FOR THE ZIG ZAG PRINCIPLE

"Entrepreneurs, you need not fear failure anymore! With *The Zig Zag Principle* in hand, you will have all the tools you need to increase your probability of success the instant you apply the concepts in the book."
—**Rick Sapio**, founder and CEO of Mutual Capital Alliance, Inc.

"*The Zig Zag Principle* isn't feel-good fluff—it is a logical and practical formula that you can put your hands on, and it will increase the rate of success of any business you apply it to."
—**Moe Abdou**, principal and founder, 33 Voices

"*The Zig Zag Principle* is more powerful than the 'release and iterate' mentality that is so prevalent today. I have adjusted my planning to incorporate this principle in our product launches. Properly executed, *The Zig Zag Principle* will keep folks like me out of financial hot water."
—**David McInnis**, founder of PRWeb.com; founder and CEO of Cranberry LLC, Venture Partners

"Most entrepreneurs find it complicated and difficult to build their businesses. Rich has done a masterful job with *The Zig Zag Principle* to make complex things simple and difficult things easy—and it works! It will help you get where you want to be with more confidence and certainty."
—**Murray Smith**, *New York Times* bestselling author of *The Answer;* CEO of MainStreetMentor.com

"Whether you are a parent, an entrepreneur, a factory worker, or a middle manager, *The Zig Zag Principle* will provide you with a framework and a formula that will empower you to make changes in your world you had never felt were possible."

—**Joseph Grenny**, *New York Times* bestselling co-author of
Influencer: The Power to Change Anything

"*The Zig Zag Principle* delivers the epiphany of the decade for business owners. These strategies are nonintuitive, but proven to be solid and dependable, which is why this is such an important work. Not only will you profit faster than you thought possible, you'll also enjoy greater balance and fulfillment in the process."

—**Leslie Householder**, award-winning bestselling author of
The Jackrabbit Factor: Portal to Genius

"I don't believe entrepreneurship is something you can truly learn from a book. Everyone has to make their own mistakes. Nevertheless, if you've already made some mistakes, then you'll find *The Zig Zag Principle* to be a no b.s. guide to starting, nurturing, and succeeding at entrepreneurship."

—**Jeffrey Eisenberg**, *New York Times* and
Wall Street Journal bestselling author of
Call to Action and Waiting for Your Cat to Bark?